P's & Q's

The journey to becoming Prime Quality

Recognizing, exercising
and utilizing your potential to
become your greatest self

CRAIG D. GLOVER HINES

PING Revelations

ISBN-13: 978-1985286207

Author Photograph: Marcus J. Williams
(Instagram: mvrcu.s)

Printed in the United States of America

DEDICATED to my hero,
Thomas Alton Glover, Jr.

FOREWORD

My son, Craig Dushay Hines, has overcome obstacles and stereotypes that have proven to hold back and hold down young men and women. Individuals from the same neighborhoods and background; labeled with stereotypes that tell distorted messages of being a product of their environment; messages that can subject them to an automatic mental prison sentence with an outcome that leads to nothing, but physical failure.

My son's work is a testament to what can be accomplished by an individual who refused to settle and who pushed pass the bonds that hold those that do. It takes two, to stop the cycle of recidivism at its first leg, within a family or between father and son.

Inspiration comes in many forms. A son can be inspired by his father's transition from a negative lifestyle to a positive outlook on life. A father can be inspired by a son who has listened to his advice, ensuring the decisions he's made doesn't reflect the mistakes of his father's past. Craig listened, Craig took it all in, and Craig applied the wisdom and understanding that comes with experience and life. I have always wanted more out of life for Craig so where he was concerned, I applied extra attention and guidance, with my life and mistakes as examples. My son has become the man that can make a difference in the lives of people. His inner spirit makes him stand out, no matter where he goes or what room he enters. God truly uses him. This is manifested in his writings.

Blessings come from God but you have to be able to recognize them and appreciate them for their worth. If one were to look at Craig's life, and the people that are around him, they would see the positive factors that play a role in influencing him. He'll tell you that I assisted in raising him over the phone and I'll counter; saying, all I did was guide and advise him over the phone. To be as smart and self-conscious at his age, and going in the direction that he's headed, it was more than phone conversations that makes him the man that he is.

Experience is the teacher of life and it doesn't always have to be your own personal experiences. To take the set of examples of a father whether negative or positive and apply them to your life so that it makes you better and helps you grow toward a goal in a world where you only get one chance to live — this is what *P's & Q's The Journey To Becoming Prime Quality* is all about.

I'm beyond proud of my son; his growth in life and the direction he is going. He is considered to be a Golden Man, someone who is not afraid of commitment or responsibility; someone that has goals set for himself and most of all someone that cherishes his family.

Growing up, while I was away in prison, Craig had two father figures in his life, his grandfather and stepfather. He will tell you, "I always told him" and his "grandpa always showed him." I stayed and continue to stay in his ear with encouragement, guidance, and support in anything he decides to take on in life. His grandpa was the one that showed him the way to carry himself and to be a man of his word. The one thing that we both made sure Craig knew is that whatever he put into something, that's what he will get out of it. So if he puts in a hundred percent then he will get that back. With this book, Craig has done just that because he knows no other way. The message is here in these pages and in order to fully understand and accept that message you must understand the mind, heart and soul of the man behind the words that fill these pages.

Regardless of the walls and barbed wire that continues to separate us; our spirits do have a divine link created by God that is fueled by love. We inspire each other in many ways and this book will inspire those that read it. Craig has come very far at such a young age, and he is gifted with insight and the inner strength that few possess. Craig has always inspired me through the life that he lives, this book even further inspires me. Craig always tells me to never break and always build. I have come to the realization that Craig has never broken regardless of his circumstances, but rather he is steadily building. *P's & Q's The Journey To Becoming Prime Quality* is one more building block to Craig's journey toward recognizing, exercising, and utilizing his potential to become his greatest self.

—Craig Hines
Inmate Number: 19322-083

"For I know the plans that
I have for you," declares the Lord,
"plans to prosper you
and not to harm you,
plans to give you hope and a future..."

—Jeremiah 29:11 (NIV)

PROLOGUE

Early one morning, on the pier of purpose, two souls sat in the stillness of serenity. Admiring everything that their heart could absorb, they listened closely. So closely, they could hear the clouds as they moved. So deeply, they could hear seeds cracking in the soil and shells singing in the sand. So intently, they could even hear the beat of their own heart. The sound was so pure that it had to be diluted with a decision; a decision to speak. One of the souls had a conviction come over him that altered the beat of his heart just a bit. The conviction was telling him, to speak first. Before he spoke, he prayed. He prayed and asked God to speak through him. He continued to pray and asked God to allow his transparency to transform him. He prayed and asked God that whatever may take place, may it fulfill the Will that He has for his life and may the desires of his heart be aligned with the will of God. He prayed to be in a constant posture of submission to God and asked that his ways be prosperous. He then prayed and asked God to open up his heart, as the hEARt is where the ear and hearing abides; so he could hear everything intended for him. His name was Potential, and he concluded his prayer with "Yet not my will, but Thy will be done."

He took a leap of faith and spoke, but to whom was he speaking? Well of course, it was Mr. Prime, that other soul that sat in the stillness of serenity. Mr. Prime that other soul who was one with Potential. Mr. Prime the one who had "been there", "done that." Mr. Prime; full of wisdom, full of grace, bound by forgiveness and freed by a heart flowing with the spirit of understanding. Mr. Prime he who had known mercy and been the recipient of countless blessings. Mr. Prime he who was clothed in unmeasurable faith.

Two purpose-filled souls; one having demonstrated potential, one in the process of being primed to reach his greatest potential. Their spirits connected and the conversation begins.

Season 1
Fall

"TRIPLE OG"
(GEORGETOWN,
GTOWN,
GLOVERSTOWN)

WHAT IF

M r. Prime, how do I reach my greatest self? What do I do? Where do I go? How do I maintain? How do I survive? How fast do I go? Mr. Prime, what if I fail? What if I get lost? What if I lose? What if my best isn't good enough? What if pain beats me down and paralyzes me? Mr. Prime, how do I stay afloat when the currents of life try to pull me under? I'm scared, Mr. Prime. I don't know how to do this.

I'm not a kid anymore, my tests are harder, my pain is different. Success isn't what they described it to be, it's much different. Mr. Prime, confusion gets to me, frustration gets to me, life gets to me. What about my dreams, Mr. Prime? Do I chase them? Do I trust them? What if I die, Mr. Prime?

Mr. Prime smiles and says to Potential, if you always wonder "what if", you'll never know "what is."

Mr. Prime pauses for a minute and sits in silence. He can hear the sound of Potential's purpose as it echoes through the pathways of promise that point in the direction of his prime. Mr. Prime gets very excited because he knows this route extremely well. He then suggest that Potential sharpen his point because there is a lot to write down. He tells him to keep a pencil instead of a pen because errors are a part of this process, which only bring purpose to the eraser.

As I talk to you don't anticipate using the eraser because that means you're expecting to mess up. Instead, allow your faith to show you that a tree is in your hand and you are simply sketching on the skies of your soul and sowing seeds on the pastures of your prime. Last but not least, if your point gets dull or is about to break, never forget that it is the sharpening that keeps you on point.

Intrigued by their conversation and connection and bound with his innate responsibility to provide guidance and direction, infused with the Spirit of God, Mr. Prime continues...

Life is a journey, especially when walking with God. It's almost like you never arrive but you constantly reach, see, strive, and learn that He always has more. There are so many different finish lines in the marathon of life. You persistently strive toward your goals, dreams, aspirations, and destinations, realizing that every plateau propels you to a new peak. As you run through one ribbon of victory, another race immediately begins. It's a forever developing story that has multiple plots and countless levels of understanding. As you constantly circle around completion, you steadily grow in enlightenment and understanding of self. You practice and practice and may never get it perfect, but you continuously improve until you eventually get it right.

The journey requires faith, discipline, knowledge, wisdom, patience, and so many other qualities that are developed over time. It's a process that you progress through. The journey has shown and continues to prove that informing isn't limited to just words, but more so a person's actions and example. A lot of people automatically assume that when you are anointed, called, or have a heart for ministry that you are called to preach or have your own church. That, however, is not the case.

Dr. Jamal Harrison Bryant, Pastor and Founder of the Empowerment Temple AME Church says "ministry is connected to a much bigger tentacle than that, it is MORE than you can imagine." In other words, ministry can be your circle and everyone and everything that you are connected to and through. Life shows you that you don't need a congregation to have a conversation. As we talk you'll see how conversations are the breeding grounds for revelations. A long conversation can renovate the soul, a short conversation can renovate the mind, but the right conversation can renovate your heart.

With many different stages of learning and instructions in life, our conversation will revolve around the ones that will help you tap into all that is inside of you. As a believer, I know that there is nothing new under the sun, and the majority of the time someone has already laid out a blueprint of how to do something or how something can be done. With a blueprint already provided, that gives you the chance to do it the right way while at the same time the chance to put your own spin on it. No one's relationship with God is the same, so never be afraid to exercise your originality and creativity. God gave us perspective not to compromise His word, but the mandate to maximize it. Your source of inspiration may be different than anything before and that in fact is the beauty, depth, and uniqueness of who you are. You are what makes you. Faith requires an imagination.

ARRESTED AT THE ARCC

A s Potential's pencil flows, his mind wants more. His captivation is driving his curiosity. He follows up with a question, Mr. Prime, talk to me about who you looked up to? How did you find your way?

Coming up, I used to ride shotgun with my grandfather, we went everywhere together. A lot of times we would just ride through DC going different places. My great grandmother used to live on 14th & T Street, SE, and we used to go over there to cut her grass and tidy her house. Other times we may ride to a doctor's appointment for him that may have been downtown somewhere. As a kid I never knew how to navigate my way around the city streets, I never had a worry to do so because I was with my grandfather.

The DC streets were just overwhelming to me, it was no way I could remember how to get somewhere. One ways here (depending on the time of day), street parking there; nothing helped me learn it quickly, and since we didn't live in DC, I wasn't going in and out of it daily, to study it. Nonetheless, my grandfather used to always tell me that one day I would learn my way around the city. "Pop, I don't know how to get there." He would respond, "You have to read signs, it's mostly all alphabets and numbers." Easy for him to say, he grew up in DC; his whole life born and raised, and here I was a suburban kid whose sense of direction to this very day still isn't great. Even still, my grandfather always assured me that "One day, you'll learn your way around the city."

Potential chimes in for a second, grandparents are special, and that's a beautiful thing to have a relationship with your grandfather like that. It's clear he had an influence and heavy impact on you, tell me more. How is he now?" Mr. Prime answers, well, I haven't seen him in a while, but I hear from him often.

In 2012, we were separated by the inevitable, but forever joined by the eternal. That year I endured a trial that really carried me to a higher place. The sky looked like the 'God Smile'. I was in my senior year at Mount Saint Mary's University in Emmitsburg, Maryland and getting a workout in with one of my friends named Charles who I nicknamed 'Chuck Buck'. Chuck Buck was from Yonkers, New York. Chuck and I had grown to be pretty close especially during my junior and senior year. We both played on the club basketball team and played ball pretty often together at the gym. As we grew closer, working out became the norm so on this particular day we went across the street from the main campus to the Knott Athletic Recreation Convocation Complex; better known to locals as the ARCC. The ARCC facility had fields behind it where we would run and do sprints.

Over time while working out and talking, Chuck became aware of my grandfather's health complications and I eventually grew to learn from Chuck that his grandfather passed away some years ago. He shared with me how he was very close, as well, to his grandfather.

It's sort of odd and ironic that Chuck and I had really deepened our bond around the time of my grandfather's decline in health, but on this day after our workout, the aura of the atmosphere just felt different. This was a Thursday, specifically, November 29. It was around 4 or 5pm when my attention was drawn to the sky; God's handy-work/God's daily drawing. The sun was setting and the sky was sort of pink with light tents of orange. It felt like the elements of nature, i.e., just the way things looked, were speaking to me: the sunset, the slight breezes, the temperature. While still on the field, I called my mom and told her that I was coming down to Georgetown Hospital that night to visit with my grandfather. I just had an urge or push of some sort that was arresting my spirit. I didn't care what was on my agenda; I had to go down there to see him that night.

As we started walking back to my dorm, I shared with Chuck that I was heading to Georgetown that night and I would pretty much see him when I got back. I went back to my room to shower and grab some food so I could start my drive down the road. Pushing my way down Highway 15, listening to this backyard CD that stayed in my CD player for so long, pretty much being the soundtrack for that season of my life. While driving down and listening to those familiar tunes, I was on my normal weekly route to Georgetown Hospital. As I made my way there in about an hour or so, I parked on the normal side-street right off of Reservoir Road.

Heading into the hospital, to the 6th floor I went. When I got up there I saw my mom, grandmother, and one of my great aunts. I think it was my Aunt Joyce or my Aunt Lois, I can't quite recall which one. I sat at the table talking to them for a while, until I eventually got up to head to the back to see my grandfather. At this stage in his sickness, he had been unconscious for some time so conversation and dialogue was out of the question. I had to find contentment in simply seeing him, touching him, and talking to him without getting a response.

There's a part of his hand that I used to touch so much when visiting him that if I position my hand a certain way and touch it, it triggers instant memories of being there with him. On this night, I had some moments with him, and was able to just reflect some at his bedside not knowing that would indeed be my last night beside him while he was breathing. As visiting hours approached their cut off time, I had weird feelings, but I did my normal. I leaned over and touched his head and told him in his ear "I love you and I just want to thank you for everything you ever did for me," and once again told him, "I love you." As I walked out of the room that night, things just felt different. I looked over my shoulder and caught one last look at the side of his face as he laid there helpless, breathing heavy and being assisted by the machine.

Even as I express my pain to you Potential, I see how pain constantly produces deeper purpose for one's life. You'll learn how pain plays a major part in the production of your prime and you'll see how it has the powerful ability to make your passions make a promise to you. It will make you never give up on what your soul was created for because it would hurt you forever if you did. It grants access to the special areas in your heart, where everything that you truly care about exists. In essence, pain only makes your purpose more clear.

Passing by it with fresh memories, I remember the café in Georgetown that I visited so frequently during the months of visiting my grandfather--as I left out that night and went to walk my mom and grandma down to the garage, I hugged them and told them both that I would let them know once I was safely back at school. Heading back to my car, walking up that familiar side street, I got in my car and heard that familiar backyard CD and pulled out of a parking lot, a "place" where I had been "parked" for months. After I made it back to the dorm, I called my mom to let her know that I was good, I went to bed and went on with my normal routine.

4REAL?

I t was Friday morning, November 30, 2012, and I was figuring out how I would spend my day, with my grandfather heavily on my mind. My roommates, Tysean and Jon were two of my dearest friends; they are like brothers to me. We were doing laundry and they told me they were going over to the ARCC to play ball for a while and asked me if I was coming. I told them, probably not, I was just going to finish my laundry and grab something to eat.

It's crazy how the setting for what was about to happen formed itself without me even knowing. So around 4:00-4:15 my mom called. During this season I was nervous to answer the phone because I never knew when the call would be 'that call'. I answered the phone, hearing screaming and agony in the background and my mother crying; she uttered the words...the words that I so dreaded. The words that I feared, but knew would someday fill the atmosphere, "Craig, Pop passed. He is gone."

After a few seconds of silence, my response was bland and probably the greatest display of painful silence ever. All I could say was..."4Real?" Not like, oh it really happened? But more like, I can't believe it.

What haunted us for months finally happened, it literally happened. Growing up I used to fear death so much, I couldn't even bear the thought of losing one of my family members because I love them so much. I had never experienced losing an immediate family member, let alone one whose bedroom was right beside mines in the house. I used to pray to God and literally say, "God just don't take my grandfather first." I used to think that I had to be warmed up to something like that, like let me experience grief in a couple other ways with some other people before something like that happens because I honestly didn't know how I would or could deal with it.

I don't even know if my body fully registered the news, all I could hear was my mom crying and the sound of that pain is still fresh. I got off the phone by saying; okay, I'm coming home.

As I hung up, it hit me; the hardest strike of my life, as if my knees buckled and air rushed out of my lungs. All of the pictures on my bulletin board in my dorm room of my grandfather only made things worse; the grief in that moment stands alone. I was alone in my bedroom crying to the point where it was difficult to breathe, staring at the pictures all around me, my mind going so fast just remembering everything we had and have done and to know that he was gone was unbearable. Nothing in my life at that point had hurt like that.

I began calming myself down and settling down barely enough to get myself together. I knew I had to go home, but I really was thinking, wow, man I'm existing in the world and my grandfather is no longer in it.

While packing my bags and getting things together, still holding back tears, I heard the door to our dorm room open and it was Tysean, he had just got his dinner and was sitting on the couch eating. Before I left, I looked at him and said "he's gone." Tysean had a look on his face that was blank and I didn't realize until later, years later, that his first response was the same as mine…a really blank, hurt, reflection of disbelief. His response: "4Real?" In an impenetrable silence; at a loss for words, Tysean got up and hugged me as I left out and headed home.

I JUST WANT MY 'POP POP' BACK, THAT'S ALL

Only God carried me down that highway that day. It was not my own strength that allowed me to drive home to Clinton, Maryland. Driving the car where I used to ride in the passenger seat, with my granddad driving, every memory was speeding through my brain. I could not get rid of the memories. All I could see was his face, remembering his smell, hearing his voice, just remembering my life with him.

Getting home to a house full of family was consoling because I couldn't imagine being alone. I was concerned for my immediate family and couldn't fathom the thought of them being alone. It was such a hard time for everyone, my mother being the only child, and losing her rock, her Daddy. My grandmother losing her husband of 50 years and my little brother, Amir, aka Mir, just turning 7 years old at the time, dealt with it the best he could based on his understanding. Amir just missed his "Pop Pop" and wanted him back.

My stepdad Anthony, aka Ant, was consoling my mother while still grieving himself; having grown close to a man that was not merely his father-in-law, but one who had become a real father figure to him. I relayed the news to my dad through email, but I could see and feel in my dad's response that it killed him. My dad has told me that my grandfather was literally like his dad and he grew to love him dearly. Those next few days were just mind numbing and strikingly cold and solemn.

My grandfather was my everything. He was a man of God, a man of principle, and a man of faith. He taught me how to ride my bike, how to drive, how to tie a necktie, always told me to be respectful and to always, always mind my manners. He would make sure my clothes and suits looked neat, told me to always do right, told me to read and no matter what get my education. He fed me, clothed me, took me to the zoo when I was younger, took me to my football and basketball practices and games, attended my track meets, took me to all of my job interviews, and he loved me unconditionally.

Full of compassion, covered in calmness, and always understanding, my grandfather was the epitome of selflessness. A man who always said the least, but always did the most. My older cousin referred to him at his funeral as the "quiet giant." I was so grateful to have him as my "Pop."

My life has definitely been different since he passed, to say the least. I honestly don't know if there was anything that he would not have done for me. But honestly, it wasn't the things that my grandfather did for me that made me love him so much. Instead it was the great amount of time we spent together during the first 21 years of my life.

His presence alone is one of the greatest things I've ever had the pleasure of embracing and experiencing. He had a pleasant aura, very peaceful and chill. He'd laugh and talk with you, he was just very mellow and gentleman-like, with an old timers' swag. He might have on a pair of corduroys with some dirty bucks and a nice blazer, or a Hanes white tee, some shorts, and his Reeboks, working out in the yard trimming the hedges or cutting the grass with his gold Cadillac chain around his neck; or his "Skins" jacket when the winter months hit. Nine times out of ten you could catch him with his tobacco pipe in his mouth.

He knew the definition of hard work but he never preached on it with words, instead his loudest words were his actions and his actions truly defined his character. We did everything together; this man was my best friend. Sitting around watching sports, eating crabs together, laughing with the family, riding with him to the doctor, and just being on his hip. He showed me so much and was a real example of love through action. He left me a compass that helped me find my way through the city.

* RiCk RiSDY*

PRIME QUALITY

Potential sits and listens as his heart is touched and without realizing or even knowing; his perspective is expanding. He parts his lips and asks, "Mr. Prime how did you heal? Have you healed? How has your hurt not stopped you?

Mr. Prime responds, that is why you are great Potential, because you engage the heart and mind with your questions. Your questions point towards purpose but pain makes you look for proof in other places, instead of looking and finding it within yourself. Potential, you are developed in pain and you are matured through the process. A person's prime is powerful only because they went through numerous processes to become the greatest version of who they are. Potential, I listen to you in amazement because it's astounding to hear you ask me questions when you are actually a great teacher all by yourself. I encourage you to use your hurt to help because life will show you how in every disappointment, there is direction.

As Mr. Prime is reminded of something God showed him earlier in his life, he says, so, Potential, a while ago you asked me, how can you become your greatest self. Mr. Prime says softly... "It all changed when he saw his own wings."

I want you to imagine living your entire life on the ground, never knowing that you could fly. How excited do you think you would be when you found out you had wings and you could soar?

If we only knew what was really inside of us.

A lot of us have king potential but a pawn mentality. In other words, we may hear about what we can potentially do but we are completely clueless about the value we have. We've been told that if we reach the fullness of our potential then we can be anything we want, but so many of us don't see or believe our value enough to truly pursue it.

The goal in life is to not only plant seeds of purpose, but also uproot the weeds that have poisoned or could possibly poison your potential. We must plant the seed if it hasn't been planted, and water it, if it already has.

You can cultivate it, but only God can elevate it. You not only have purpose, you also have promise. Focus on seeing your substance and understanding your significance. God created you with providential promise, purpose, and position; a divine destiny, and an authorized assignment. To be blessed in such a way means there is much required.

I know that if young men like yourself and young women were constantly bombarded with positivity, always told and shown about their potential, gifts, abilities, and what they could be, that would then catapult them into a stage of confidence, belief, and action. They would become passionate about reaching their prime.

Potential listens deeply to what Mr. Prime is telling him. The words are starting to not only resonate with his mind and heart, but are traveling to levels he didn't quite know existed. Potential's heart became overwhelmed and his mouth began to bleed question after question after question.

Did your grandfather teach you about all of that Mr. Prime? Mr. Prime, what provokes your spirit to process things like this? Mr. Prime, how do you define your prime?

The questions from Potential are starting to have a similar effect on

Mr. Prime. Their conversation deepens and Mr. Prime continues... My grandfather, the late Thomas Alton Glover used to tell me, "P's & Q's" every time I left the house. Little did I know that phrase would serve as the biggest motivator in my life. As he would define it, it simply means to be on your best behavior, mind your manners, be respectful, and do the right thing. Listen, Potential, this conversation with you truly honors my grandfather because everything I am saying to you is essentially my answer, explanation, and account of what it takes to reach your *Prime Quality* in life.

So then neither is he that planteth any thing,
neither he that watereth;
but God that giveth the increase.
Now he that planteth and he that watereth are one:
and every man shall receive his own reward
according to his own labour.

— 1 Corinthians 3:7-8 (KJV)

THE DOUBTERS DANCE

Mr. Prime deepens the discussion and informs Potential that life is the real school and we as people are broken down into stages, segments, and seasons and we are students who learn every single day. Some days we have quizzes, other days we have tests, some days there might be a pop quiz while other days may involve a group project. You may be running behind some days, get in trouble, have to serve a detention or penalty of some sort...life is a school. We are forever learners because even when we teach, we learn.

The beautiful blessing about life though is God does not weigh and view us off our GPA. His grace allows us to sometimes fail, and still be able to receive a lesson so we can move to the next grade in life. Every time we go to the next grade we graduate higher into the next level of who we were created to be. Grace has the power to grant you your ticket to graduation.

My grandfather was born on June 26, 1936, in Washington, DC, and raised in the Garfield neighborhood. He grew up in a much different era than the one we currently live in, so the morals and principles that he grew up on and taught me have honestly faded out some over the years.

Nevertheless, they still hold the same substance, truth, and life that they held in his heyday. I grew stronger and learned so much from his passing; it is almost as if he still teaches me lessons while deceased. It was ever so often when I would hear him say "P's & Q's." I would have never guessed that this simple phrase that he uttered to me so often would be the phrase that impacted my life beyond measure.

P's and Q's is about constructing yourself properly while striving to reach your Prime Quality, aka your best self. It's about striving to be the best individual you can be. It's about being respectful at all times; to parents, peers, others' perspectives, yourself and God. It's about representing your family and representing God in how you live. It's about having manners and doing the simple things well. It's about overcoming obstacles and growing to appreciate adversity. It's about believing in yourself. Most importantly, it's about doing the right thing because you want to and choose to. This means not only doing the right thing while being seen, but making the right choices even when no one is looking and more so making the right choices even if you won't get recognized or be given credit for it.

My grandfather, would say that P's and Q's certainly does mean "prime quality." Prime is a triple threat. It is a noun, verb, and an adjective; meaning it is something, it does something, and it describes something. According to Dictionary.com, Prime is "the period or state of greatest perfection or vigor of human life," it is the process of preparing or making ready for a particular purpose or operation, and it is of first importance; demanding the fullest consideration. Prime is simply the best.

Quality is defined as a high level of value or grade of excellence. It is a high grade of superiority (a grade of fineness) and together they define the late Thomas Alton Glover. Your prime quality is you doing your best even when you're not at your best, all while constantly becoming your best. These teachings are the manifestations of the man that I am today, the man that I am becoming, and the message I aim to deliver due to my grandfather's insistence that I stay on my P's and Q's.

I believe young men should learn and know many things in order to reach their best self. It must be their faith, their mindset (outlook), how they love themselves, how they respect themselves, their ability to plan and ability to execute, their actions, their speech, their attire, their character, their ability to listen, ability to serve, ability to love, humility, confidence, and their nonstop constant pursuit, desire and passion to unlock every possible secret there is to fulfilling their purpose in life. My grandfather exemplified these things, and I thank God I was a student to his life.

Reaching your prime quality is something that doesn't just take place once, it's not like you just run through the finish line and say I'm done or I've arrived. That's not how it works.

In your life you will run through many different finish lines because as soon as you run through one, another race immediately begins. Life has a way of showing you the importance of pacing yourself and appreciating the process of preparing for each race and striding your way through them. Although you may have to sprint at times, we learn from life and the Word of God that the race is not given to the strong nor the swift, but to those who can endure until the end. Life is a journey and your prime quality is what you discover along the way.

There will always be something you didn't know, something you didn't do, someone you haven't met, an opportunity for growth, a way to get better, more people to help, more love to give, more love to receive. However, as you go and grow on this journey you will encounter many different types of people, visit many different places, encounter many problems, live through many experiences and they will all contribute to who you are. Each and every day you will get better, and learn more than you did the day before. Learning is inevitable. If you live then you will learn. More importantly, it's the application of the things we learn that will show us the significance of the places we've been, the people we've met, the problems we've overcome, and the things we've lived through on our journey through life.

Consider what the legend Bruce Lee said...

"If you always put limits on what you can do, physical or anything else, it'll spread over into the rest of your life. It'll spread into your work, into your morality, into your entire being. There are no limits. There are plateaus, but you must not stay there, you must go beyond them. If it kills you, it kills you. A man must constantly exceed his level. There is no such thing as maturity; there is instead an ever-evolving process of maturing. Because when there is a maturity, there is a conclusion and a cessation. That's when the coffin is closed. You might be deteriorating physically in the long process of aging, but your personal process of daily discovery is ongoing. You continue to learn more and more about yourself every day."

In essence, maturity is never reached because maturation happens every day. A man can't fathom the things that God has for him nor can He imagine the things that God can do through him. We never know how far He will take us or where he will take us. Maturation is not a destination, it is a journey.

You have to test yourself and try yourself daily with the sole intention of bettering who you are. The ultimate level of confidence is when you understand the importance of competing with yourself without condemning yourself. You are your biggest competition and you are your toughest opponent. As you pursue your prime quality you'll see that the only way it is attainable is by going, and growing, while you go. Each day you live bettering yourself, making changes, making decisions, recovering from mistakes, learning, helping, listening, and doing things that help improve who you are. This process is your prime quality. In simplest terms, you become something when you realize you never stop becoming it.

Your prime quality is when you realize that you're constantly maturing into more and more of who you are. When you get to a state of such fruitfulness where you plant seeds without digging holes, you simply can just drop the things that are in your hands because the grounds that God has ordered your steps on are so rich and fertile they can only produce glory. Your prime quality is a state of fullness, where you know who fills you up and your overflow blesses other people. As you help others see things on their journey, this ultimately helps you see more on yours. Helping someone else can sometimes provide you with the clarity you need and sometimes the encouragement you need is exactly what you tell others. Again, this is not a place you just arrive at, the journey is the gateway to this place and it goes forever. Your life is the pathway to your promise. Your life is the path to your purpose. Your life is your journey, and you become your best while pursuing your prime quality. Live, believe, and love at your best because your prime is when love becomes your way of life.

Potential listens as his heart and mind are now on one accord. The synchrony between the two make his soul sing. He feels as if something he always knew, is now only beginning to be understood.

Potential has always had vision but his eyesight is where his weakness resided. His spirit has always understood what his mind is now beginning to learn. But in this moment he feels like glasses have been put on the eyes of his soul and clarity is being fed to his call. He thinks of the things that have been said to him and instead of having more questions for Mr. Prime, he sits in silence and thinks about all the mistakes he has made. He wonders to himself...what about my mistakes?

Mr. Prime can hear Potential's process as it steadily increases in power. It sounds like a concert with a passionate performance from his favorite band called "belief." Mr. Prime parts his lips and says to Potential, soon doubt will not be able to contain you. But for now, I'll answer what you asked in silence. Potential responds, "How do you know what I wanted to ask? Mr. Prime says, "Because the band of belief has a distinct power to always make 'The Doubters Dance'."

THE CUTTING

Mr. Prime continues...

Respect a person by listening to them. If you listen to them, they can reach you. If they can reach you, they can teach you. If they can teach you, they can learn from you. If they can learn from you, they will respect you. You'll never fully learn from something, someone, or yourself until you respect it, them, and you. When you value your own life and respect yourself first, you can then truly value someone else and respect them. Respect for others reciprocates self-respect and self-respect reciprocates respect for others.

The barbershop is a place where I learned about respect. A community (Common Unity) of men with a special craft; all having different styles and perspectives, but could unify together to create an atmosphere to always make you leave better than you came. The things you do for God last forever, but the things you do for self-have an expiration date. That's just an example of the many things I've learned in the barbershop.

When you hear the word respect, what is it that first comes to mind? Is it listening, staying quiet or doing what you believe to be correct? Is it knowing when to hold it and when to fold it? Is it the decision to keep your mouth shut if you have nothing nice to say? Is it treating people how you would want to be treated? Is it giving someone eye contact when they are speaking to you? Is it being honest even when it's not popular? I would say it involves all of those things to a degree but there is in fact an extension to the definition of the term. When I think of respect, I think of simply doing what is right and treating people right. I think it is caring about yourself and other people.

When you respect someone you naturally, but consciously, make decisions that take that person's preferences, feelings, and best interest into consideration. I think it is doing things that others might consider crazy, but you do it because you uphold values and morals even if they aren't common. This shows that you respect yourself enough to care about yourself and you respect other people enough to care about them. Respect is a language of love that conveys compassion, honesty, accountability and concern for another person. Respect is never rude and it is always right because respect has a tone that never offends. It knows how to approach the unapproachable. It cares about the results, which makes it adhere to the procedures of one's process. Respect sees the worth in people and admires the value in all things. Respect is when you have regard for someone else even if there is no reward for you. Without respect you are incomplete. It cost a person nothing to respect another individual, but the moment you disrespect someone, it indeed comes with a cost. Sometimes it's a price that may be more expensive than you can afford. It could end up costing you someone's trust, your reputation, maybe even life in some extreme cases.

When one has respect, he enables himself to be able to listen and be attentive to those around him. Respect for others expands the dimensions of your perspective, while respect for yourself keeps those dimensions aligned with your own moral boundaries. Respect is the key to many opportunities and sets the playing field in your favor. If you have respect and manners, a lot will miss you, but if you don't a lot will hit you. Respect is essential to the character of a person. It is a common ingredient in the character of people. Some lack it while others have the perfect amount of it, but you can never have too much of it. If character is an outfit, respect should be a part of your daily wardrobe.

The barbershop taught me the importance of grooming and neatness of not just one's appearance, but one's character. Men have to get more than just their hairline shaped up. The clippers honestly serve as a symbol to show how cutting is critical for the construction of one's character. It does a man no good if the outside is sharp and on point, but the inside is dull; lacking respect and integrity. A haircut is more than a fade, box, temple taper, shave, or beard trim. It's the cutting away of the unnecessary, ultimately to present your best self and your strongest look.

A lot of times we may underestimate our own strengths and capabilities which in some cases lead to a stage of stagnancy and complacency. For example, when you're in the barber chair, at the end of your cut the barber hands you the mirror to show you the results. When he hands you the mirror it's so you can see the final product of what was being worked on. That simple respectful act of the barber showing you the results at the end of the cut shows you that you don't reach results until you get the cut first. Results are heavily determined by the procedures, the product comes after the process, and correction comes after conviction. Results come after some work has been put in. When you go in the barbershop, you go in with the intention of coming out better than you arrived and the action that leads to that 'better you' is "the cutting."

A real man acknowledges his weaknesses and works on them. A real man has enough self-respect to make self-improvements. Don't be afraid to cut off the unnecessary. The enemy studies you. You have to develop and strengthen what he thinks is weak. We give so many things permission to hang on to us when in fact they are prohibiting us from reaching our destiny. Constructing your character will inevitably involve cutting. Don't be afraid to get cut.

"As iron sharpens iron, so one man sharpens another.
[And influences] another [through discussion]."

—Proverbs 27:17 (AMP)

Season 2 Winter

THE BARBERSHOP

PAINFUL & PERSONAL

Sometimes you have to be your own iron because your faith is maximized when you have to go against yourself. Being your own iron simply means, sometimes you have to cut yourself or be willing to do the things that will cut you, but in the end compliment you.

The things that are detrimental to your development and destiny are things you must be willing to cut off. Consider the circumcision of Abraham. Clearly, your faith has to be on a very peculiar level if you can do this to yourself. What exactly was the purpose of this? Why did God want him to inflict that type of physical pain on himself? How difficult is it for someone to make a decision that will elevate them, but hurt them at the same time? Very difficult, I'd say. Tribulation always comes before elevation but pain can make you blind to that and not just on a spiritual level, but even on a practical level.

Trusting God is sometimes extremely painful. If anyone tries to argue with you on that, tell them to go read the book of Job. Trusting God sometimes hurts! However, your purpose and prime is not attainable without pain. God has shown and told us that there are some things that we are going to have to go through that are extremely difficult and very painful. The worst part is this, some of that stuff, you're going to have to do, to yourself. Self-respect leads to self-rectification and real conviction leads to self-infliction. Why? Because affliction is a part of your anointing and correction is necessary for your call. However, if you can trust God through the pain, the peace He will give you will show you that none of it is ever in vain.

For our light affliction, which is but for a moment, worketh for us a far more exceeding and eternal weight of glory; 2 Corinthians 4:17 KJV

If you want success and if you want to have everything that God has for you, you simply have to do things differently. When you are different you can't do the same things or think the same way because you are going to a different place. When you think you're good, get better. When you're going hard, go harder. When you get stronger, keep working. When the blessings come, keep praying. Never ever stop thanking God.

Always remember that peculiar people have peculiar problems because they have a peculiar purpose. When you are different, your tests will be different, your pain will be different, but so will your peace. Your uniqueness is what a lot of people won't understand, but never live for the understanding of others. The path God has for you is one of a kind and the relationship you have with Him is special, intimate, and personal. The more you learn about God the more you learn about you and the more you know God the more you understand about yourself. The size of your call and potential determines the intensity of your "cuts." The extremity of your trials and pain bring validity to your testimony and purpose. God has put His power in you and sometimes pain is the only thing that can get it out. When your purpose is peculiar your pain has to be personal.

Potential is growing at a nice pace and his thoughts are shifting more and more into the positive, but he still has more questions: So Mr. Prime, I'm following you on what you're saying about "cutting and getting cut" but what if so much cutting happens in my life that I just constantly bleed and it makes me weak. What if I bleed out?

CUT & CLIMB

Mr. Prime follows up, remember...A wise man constantly makes himself better. The purpose of cutting is to address your weaknesses. Your weakness stays weak (and assumes the role of power and dominance) if it isn't addressed. Every day, challenge your weaknesses by cutting and constructing your character. You will always develop more strengths when you admit where you are weak. The acknowledgment of a problem is the first step in finding a solution for it. You'll never maximize the strength of the space that God has given you if you continue to entertain weakness (your flesh). You in a sense have to make your weakness bored, and instead of entertaining it, exercise it. The goal should be to work your weakness until it becomes a strength. It's almost like climbing a rope with something tied around your ankle. The rope around your ankle can only stretch but so far which only allows you to climb to a certain point and level. The more we entertain flesh and weakness, and not exercise the spirit, the longer we have to deal with the rope around our ankle that inhibits us from getting to those higher stages in our development.

Every day you are going to a certain point, which may indeed be high, but you can only go so high because that rope is tied around your ankle preventing your further elevation. In other words you are only getting to the level that your flaws allow, not knowing that with slight corrections you would see and become so much more. You must be willing to cut yourself daily in order to convert that weakness to a point of strength. When you get that rope off of your ankle, there is nothing that can hold you back from climbing the rope of revelation.

As far as thinking that the cutting you go through will make you bleed and make you weak, that's okay. Your blood is powerful and it speaks. And don't worry about bleeding out, if that ever happens you'll be in one of the rarest realms that exist. You'll have a blood transfusion that will transform you forever.

HIS CHISEL

Consider these four Pillars (Paul, James, Kahlil Gibran, and Paulo Coelho) and their perspective on pain. The first being Apostle Paul and what he says in his letter to Corinth, "but he said to me, 'My grace is sufficient for you, for my power is made perfect in weakness.' Therefore, I will boast all the more gladly about my weaknesses, so that Christ's power may rest on me."

Second, a servant of God named James as he speaks about profiting from trials, he says, "My brethren, count it all joy when you fall into various trials, knowing that the testing of your faith produces patience. But let patience have its perfect work, that you may be perfect and complete, lacking nothing. If any of you lacks wisdom, let him ask of God, who gives to all liberally and without reproach, and it will be given to him. But let him ask in faith, without doubting, for he who doubts is like a wave of the sea driven and tossed by the wind. For let not that man suppose that he will receive anything from the Lord; he is a double-minded man, unstable in all his ways." James 1:2-8 NKJV.

Third, a legend from Lebanon named Kahlil Gibran who said that pain is the breaking of the shell that encloses your understanding.

And, fourth, Paulo Coelho, a "Warrior of the Light," who echoed John Bunyan: "Although, I have been through all that I have, I do not regret the many hardships I met, because it was they who brought me to the place I wished to reach. Now all I have is this sword and I give it to whoever wishes to continue his pilgrimage. I carry with me the marks and scars of battles-they are the witnesses of what I suffered and the rewards of what I conquered. These are the beloved scars that will open the gates of Paradise to me. There was a time when I used to listen to tales of bravery. There was a time when I lived only because I needed to live. But now I live because I am a Warrior and because I wish one day to be in the company of Him for whom I have fought so hard."

Potential, you must live your life like your prime depends on it. Live like your life depends on it. There is always higher, to go in God. He will encourage you until you enter eternity with Him which is why He will discipline you when you are heading away from your destiny. God's destiny for you is in eternity with Him and as He molds you into the sculpture that He envisions, He has to construct you with His chisel.

Your weakness could be anything, find out what it is so it doesn't damage everything. Do a great job because you want to. Be great because you want to be. Look at your life as something precious and everything you do contributes greatly to the development of it or the destruction of it. Don't condemn yourself or others. Let conviction do the construction on you. Condemnation cuts and kills, conviction cuts and corrects.

IT HAPPENS #decisions

Mr. Prime pauses for a second to listen. He can still hear waves roaring in the heart of Potential, so he raises his sail to catch the winds from his soul. I remember you asked, "What happens if I mess up?" Sometimes we make bad decisions, which, consequently lead us to make better decisions.

Every form of adversity you go through in life, is to develop and sharpen your vision. Your best days are always in front of you because everything behind you, makes you better each day. There are people all over the world who soak in the past, and are restless in regret of the things they wish they had or had not done. It's pretty much inevitable, in the process of becoming your best self and making yourself better, you will indeed at some point mess up. It happens.

FIND THE MIRACLES

Ask yourself Potential, are mistakes really failures if you learned something from them? Mistakes are messages that are meant to mold you. You're supposed to learn from what you did wrong so you won't repeat the actions that led to it. Mistakes are moments of misunderstanding that lead to times of teaching, relearning, and reapplying. Mistakes have their purpose and they are meant to teach a lesson. According to Jamal Harrison Bryant, "Mistakes qualify you for miracles and your reputation is easier kept than recovered." It's a much more stringent process to recover your reputation than to maintain it.

Let's go back to the barbershop analogy. The client is the one getting the cut and the barber is the one doing the cutting. Now barbers work on their craft daily because cutting hair is their way of practicing. What's interesting is a barber practices and performs all at the same time. They are doing their best on each client but learning more and more each time until they reach a stage of mastery with their skill. They master the art of performing because they are literally always practicing.

A barber learns his/her clients, so they know what to do each time and can make adjustments based on request. Nonetheless, there are barbers who will tell you that they've accidentally cut a patch in someone's head, cut someone's hair too low, cut their client with the clippers, or whatever it might be. The point is, at one point in time they too were in a stage where they made mistakes. But each mistake showed them what to stop doing and what to continue to do. How does this relate to life? You make mistakes until you have fully understood the lesson that the mistake was intended to teach.

Knowledge becomes wise when it is understood. Consider what Effiong, a dear friend of mine, said, *"There are no such things as mistakes, because a mistake is a lesson we've yet to understand."* So in actuality, a mistake is always a lesson, but it's only when a person understands their error that they can grow and learn from it. A mistake leaves you with knowledge but the wisdom you gain comes from your proper application of that knowledge. Sometimes God allows us to make mistakes because His knowledge will come from it. Application of God's knowledge is wisdom.

Pastor Lance Watson of the St. Paul's Baptist Church in Richmond, Virginia states that "Planning isn't as valuable as learning. And learning comes from trying. And trying inevitably involves failures." An effort to try and try hard in life will at times become a very stringent and arduous process and will in fact involve some failures. However, how can something be a failure if at the end of the day it still deposited more in you than you previously had?

There are people everywhere; including myself who have done things they know they shouldn't have done. It could be something big or small, but the point is something was done that you later thought about and said, "I could have done this differently, or could have handled the situation better. Maybe I could have been a bit more patient, maybe I could have been a bit more disciplined, maybe I could or should have listened, and maybe I could have been a bit more obedient. Maybe I could have paid closer attention, maybe I could have worked harder, maybe I shouldn't have; regardless of what it is that you have done, hindsight will always be 20/20.

If you must look back, only look to see how far God has brought you. Do not soak in the misery of your mistakes, instead, find the miracles in them.

Hindsight is always 20/20 because it always makes you see clearer than you did before. Allow your mistakes to manifest a more mature move that carries you forward. If you can't afford to pay the consequences, then your mistakes are too expensive and you should probably make another decision that you can live with. When a person lets their mistakes manifest maturity in their lives, they then enter a state when they seek to truly understand the purpose of mishaps so they can become better after them. Everyone messes up, but try to not make mistakes that you can't recover from. It's a lot easier to just go to the shop and get your oil changed when you're supposed to versus getting a new transmission or engine because you ignored the earlier signs.

There is no one on earth that has not made a mistake. You are not different because you failed and you are not a failure because you messed up. A person that has never made any mistakes, what have they learned? We are lifelong learners so taking L's is a necessary part of life.

"Don't fear failure. Not failure, but low aim, is the crime. In great attempts it is glorious even to fail." – Bruce Lee.

In fact, it is when people make some of the biggest mistakes of their lives that tends to ultimately be the stimulus of them growing closer to God and reaching their biggest achievements. We have to hurt to grow. Grief is one of the main ingredients in growth. There will be some pain on your path when pursuing your prime. However, the greatest thing about hurting is healing. Embrace your pain and let it propel you deeper into your purpose. Don't let the pain push you further away from the promises over your life. Don't let the pain make you forget the promise.

Don't let the pain make you forget about those that care about you.

Always proceed at pursuing your purpose and never let pain prevent it. Rest assured, knowing that all of what you go through is working for your good. In the midst of your work, God has already prepared your blessing. We just have to keep our character groomed because you never know when you will have an unannounced interview for elevation.

Your purpose is associated with your pain because your prosperity is not possible without it.

Mr. Prime continues by asking Potential a few questions: Could you imagine if you went through life and you never experienced any trouble? If you never got cut? You never experienced any letdowns, any mishaps, any disappointment or pain? Could you imagine if you went completely through life and never needed anyone for anything because you never lacked or you never failed? Could you imagine if you went through life and you simply never lost? If this was the case and all you did was win, how do you think you would act, react, and respond to failure or losing? What type of character do you think you would have? Losing would probably catch you by a complete surprise and since it would be something you had never experienced before, you probably wouldn't handle it in the best manner because all you know is one way and that is winning. When all you know is one route, what happens when there is traffic? You never want to be disabled because of defeat. As you live, you grow to see that it is important, to literally know how to lose.

Potential responds by saying, why should I know how to lose if all I aim to do is win?" Mr. Prime: Glad you asked.

Season 3 Spring

DEFINED & REFINED

DEFINING MOMENTS

Aiming for victory is what one should always do, no matter the task. Always seek to achieve victory, put forth a winning effort and learn while doing so. However, that does not make anyone exempt from defeats because if all you did was win, you wouldn't need God.

Losing is something that you will experience in this life, therefore, you must know how to handle defeat. If you know how to handle defeat, you'll never be defeated because when you know how to handle defeat, you never let it handle or dismantle you. When you're able to control yourself and stay composed under unfortunate circumstances; you know how to handle defeat.

Anyone can win, but who can lose? Who can lose with integrity and keep their character intact? Who can survive the attack? As ironic as it seems, in some instances, losing teaches more lessons than winning. When you take L's in life, it makes you appreciate your W's much more. When you know how a loss feels, you cherish and appreciate the process of getting to a victory much more than you normally would. A loss puts things in a different perspective because you take less for granted after you've lost something. So depending on how you look at it, you can sometimes gain more from a loss than you can from a win. The power lies in your perspective.

When competitors of any type lose, some choose not to acknowledge their competition by not displaying good sportsmanship and don't go back to the drawing board to correct their mistakes or sharpen their craft. They instead maintain a stubborn attitude, a non-coachable character, stay in their frustration and don't have enough humility to decrease their ego so they can be increased in character. On the other hand, there are athletes and competitors who always conduct themselves well, display great sportsmanship, respect their opponents, appreciate adversity, and know that without a doubt they are going 110% for the win, but if the outcome is different, they understand a loss doesn't mean they've lost. Frustration is a part of elevation and on your way up gravity does play its role. Life will appear to be pulling you down while God is steadily pulling you up. Never be comfortable with losing, but strive to always be content with your efforts of achieving greater.

Defining Moments: *"A point at which the essential nature or character of a person or group is revealed or identified."* We all experience moments in our lives that serve as bookmarks of remembrance. Success is easy to remember, but pain you seem to never forget. It's easy to remember your accomplishments, breakthroughs, awards, acknowledgments, graduations, and all other moments of achievement. Times such as these are amazing, they make you smile and they are a reason to celebrate. Success naturally produces smiles, but is usually birthed through trials. Trials are put in place for one to overcome so they can reach another level of success. You are often presented with challenges over and over again because there is always a part of your character that God wants to critique. He constantly teaches you lessons because He has an endless supply of blessings for your life. He has to constantly develop you because He is infinite. Before God grants you your certification for the next course, He wants to make sure you make the corrections, in the current one, first.

When moments of defeat occur it causes certain people to cope in different ways. Defeat and failure can stay in our minds longer than we desire. Have you ever stopped and wondered why that is? God will teach you some of the most valuable lessons on the ground because you have to learn and know them before you go up. The entire purpose of a loss, is to understand what it will take to win. However, even after understanding what it takes to win, that doesn't automatically promise victory. With the information needed to win, one can apply knowledge with the intention to win but can still fall short. Training constantly and losing constantly doesn't guarantee that a win is coming, but it creates a stronger desire for improvement. This re-emphasizes the point of never being comfortable with losing, but always content with your efforts of achieving greater. Your practice is always bigger than your performance because you have to succeed in private first before you can win in public. The private eye of God is bigger than the public eye of the world.

A learning process such as this has the potential to teach a person that contentment is good because you work hard until you reach fulfillment, however, you never become complacent in what you've done. Contentment is leaving the gym feeling good about the work you put in, but ready to give more tomorrow. Complacency is feeling satisfied with the work you put in today, believing that it will suffice for the remainder of the week. Complacency keeps you in your comfort zone because it's a sense of security. Contentment seeks fulfillment in each stage of the journey, while complacency is satisfied with just beginning.

The pursuit of your prime quality teaches you that the revelation usually comes out of tribulation, but the work you put forth accompanied with your faith is what will create the manifestation. Your defining moment comes to you when you are in the face of defeat or right after you lose. When you think about the purpose of a definition, it is to tell you what something means, however, how you handle defeat ultimately defines you.

Defeat tells you the definition of your desire. Defeat tells you how bad you want it, it defines the strength of your desires. Defeat develops you. Defeat strengthens the definition of your character. The Reverend Dr. Martin Luther King, Jr., said, "The ultimate measure of a man is not where he stands in moments of comfort and convenience, but where he stands in times of challenge and controversy."

I'll give you a perfect example...

SMOOTH JAZZ

K obe Bryant over the span of his NBA career made a total of 13,731 shots. He missed 16,966 shots. Adding up his misses and makes, with the exception of 2 shots from the 2012 – 2013 season that were not accounted for, he attempted a total of 30,699. Out of all of these shots, there are 4 in particular that stand out to me the most. They weren't all net, they weren't off the glass, free throws, or any made shot. Out of Kobe Bryant's entire career I feel his most significant shots were 4 air balls that he shot in the 1997 Western Conference Semifinals against the Utah Jazz. Potentially, one of the most deflating moments in his young career, Kobe shot 3 air balls in the final minute of overtime and four total including the final seconds of the 4th quarter. There are so many things that I find amazing about this story, but I, without question, view this as Kobe Bryant's *Defining Moment.*

In a very competitive match, against the Jazz, Kobe took on the challenge of chasing victory with no fear of failing. When fearless, faith takes even larger leaps. Having the confidence to even take the big shots is something that separates and defines different breeds.

As deflating and discouraging as these air balls could have been, they actually served a different purpose. What appeared to be discouraging and deflating in fact only deepened and defined Kobe's inner desire. "Defeat tells you how bad you want it, and it tells you the strength of your desire." That's exactly what those air balls did for

Kobe. The game ended, but Kobe's night had essentially just begun.

After the game, the Lakers flew back to LA and most players made their way home, but Kobe took a different route and was introduced to the power of the perfect combination. His frustration and determination, led him to create a new method to cope with defeat: *Frustration + Determination = One's ability to Create*. In order to overcome his frustration he was determined to exercise his creativity repeatedly.

"The whole entire purpose of a loss, is to understand what it will take to win." And I believe on this night, Kobe Bryant's understanding of this grew immensely. On that night, Kobe went to Palisades High School and he shot jump shots all night and into the morning.

As a man of faith, I don't really believe in coincidences. I do, however, believe that everything is purposed and God is the orchestrator of all things. Romans 8:28 reads, "And we know that all things work together for good to them that love God, to them who are called according to His purpose" (KJV). This man's defining moment came in his rookie season against the Utah Jazz. Now look at how wonderfully God weaves things together. In his rookie season, Kobe Bryant loss to the Utah Jazz. I feel that was his first real taste of defeat, athletically. After shooting those air balls, Kobe went back to the drawing board to work, practice, regain composure, and refocus, so he could perform better. He tasted defeat athletically, but the lesson permeates into every area of life. Kobe understood that this was part of his process.

My uncle Phillip once shared with me that there is a prepared place for prepared people. As Kobe prepared for his next opportunity, he was granted another chance to face the Utah Jazz, which came six months later at the first game of the season. Kobe scored a then-game high and highlight filled 23 points off the bench in a 104-87 win. What you thought you missed out on, God will make work for you. Now honestly, this story didn't truly awe me until this point: the 2015-2016 NBA season. Kobe announced that this would be his last season playing and that he would retire. This announcement literally shook the sports world. His announcement actually started a tour where he would visit opposing arenas for the last time. This created such an eagerness in fans who wanted to be in attendance to see him one last time. The Boston Celtics organization, in a symbolic gesture, presented Kobe with a piece of hardwood from their arena's floor, which I thought was beyond incredible. Every arena sold out all the way up until his epic, legendary, and unforgettable last game.

April 13, 2016 - Mamba Day- A day truly earned by Kobe Bryant, this would be his last time to strike. Los Angeles, California…the Staples Center had the honor to host the last game of one of their beloved icons. Friends and internet sources have said that fans were outside of the arena from the morning all the way until game time and hours after the game. As the arena filled, fans from all over the world did what they could to attend this game. Records of all sorts were broken; attendance, merchandise sales, celebrity appearances…all for the man himself, Kobe Bryant.

For twenty seasons, he put together such a remarkable body of work that it was appreciated by millions of basketball fans all across the world. I myself included. What's hilariously amazing about this story is who his very last NBA opponent was…take a guess...the Utah Jazz. Coincidence? Naw, I don't think so. It's key to know that failure can sometimes bring favor.

Leading up to this point, he went through so much pain because of injuries, poor shooting displays, a poor team record, and no playoff appearances in his last few years. But on this day, Kobe finished his career against the team that he first shot those air balls. His last performance was the total opposite of air balls, he scored 60 points as a 20 year veteran and captured his final victory with his team. He literally led them to victory. The performance was something you honestly had to witness to fully appreciate, but I mention it to show that no matter how hard defeat hits you, your desire always has the potential to hit it back harder. Defeat increases one's determination and I feel that Kobe Bryant's career is a perfect demonstration and example of this.

Don't be satisfied with defeat, instead be encouraged and motivated by your efforts as you strive to become a better version of yourself. Never be satisfied with defeat, but do your best to be content with what you put forth because losing indeed has its purpose. The process is what fulfills the purpose, and the way something is applied is what makes it positive or not. There will be times where you have to get violent with your circumstances, not necessarily with force but with a fiery passion to overcome. Once you learn how to apply your frustration and pain properly; you learn how to get the power from it. Frustration and pain themselves have a purpose, which is to drive you closer to fulfilling yours. If it is on your path, it is for your good, because for every place of pain, there's a deeper place of peace. Remind yourself that it's a reason for all of this and even in your season of "unknown" God is preparing you. You are being defined by constantly being refined. God constantly deepens your definition by teaching you through repetition. The things you thought were beating you deeper into the ground are only going to launch you higher into everything you were created to be.

GETTING IN SHAPE

I want you to understand this Potential, light afflictions are common to heavy anointing's. It is always working out for your good so you have to allow God to use you, even when it's uncomfortable. See the thing about an anointing is it can't be left alone, especially when you start living for God. Your character is critical for your call and your character is what keeps your anointing in shape. It's a reason God keeps "calling" you. God knows what He put in you and when you do your best to honor Him with what He gave you, He will test you, but with purpose. God can use anyone. But I don't believe His desire for you is to be dull because He loves you too much. This is why you go through what you go through. Even in the midst of your greatest blessings, He will be right there in the midst testing you. Why? So you stay close to Him while you reap. God loves you too much to leave you alone. Tell yourself right now and believe it in your heart right now that whatever it is that you are going through is working out for your good. There is a lesson in every blessing and a blessing in every lesson.

It's difficult when you're frustrated because it can make you want to give up and retreat back to old ways. It triggers emotions, turns smiles upside down, and sometimes can deplete desires. Frustration can make you go back and repeat bad habits because it makes one tired. Usually when someone is fatigued they go back to past ways, the bare minimum, or anything that will simply get them out, even if it's the wrong way. However, when you make it out of a situation it's then that you understand the value and purpose of the storm and how much the trial actually benefited you.

It's hard to understand, realize, and accept while in it because pain doesn't always produce visible progress. Once you make it out, you have a clearer perspective, view, and understanding of everything that took place. Losing with God is impossible because He can do anything but fail. You have to know how things look at the low points, because if you don't you won't ever get fulfilled from winning nor appreciate the view from the mountain top. The beauty of a peak is discovered in a valley.

Consider what flowed out of the spirit of a Warrior, Marcus Dixon, some years ago...

"Frustration is an indication that your situation is going through transformation."

POINT GUARDS & QUARTERBACKS

"The student is not above the teacher, but everyone who is fully trained will be like their teacher."

—Luke 6:40 (NIV)

Potential is growing…the tree in his hand is deepening its roots and his imagination is branching out.

I love sports too, Mr. Prime, I always have. Not only are they fun, but the games teach so many lessons about life. They build character and they show the power and potential of physical performance. They also provide one with a platform to be influential in deep ways. What do you love about sports the most Mr. Prime?

Mr. Prime answers by saying, I love what you said, and I honestly would say the same. I would also say that sports help build the will that is within. Sports can teach a person how to transfer their physical strength into mental strength and most importantly spiritual strength. Sports have taught me how to be physically strong, mentally stronger, but spiritually strongest. The potential of who you are as a person comes to show itself when adversity is right in your face because competition and challenges have a unique way to bring out the power that is in your call. Your physique or physical shell will grow and be able to endure things, but your mind must be strong enough to not let your body give up, all at the same time your spirit being the mortar of it all.

Mr. Prime continues…

Following the leader, keeps you in the lead and following the leader, teaches you how to lead.

The disciple is not above his master: but every one that is perfect shall be as his master. (KVJ)

Without discipline you'll never reach that next level of who you are. To become as your master, one must master the discipline phase, daily. All real leaders are disciplined. They know how and who to follow. As you learn who you are, you'll grow to know whose you are. The more you train with your master, the more He shows you how to master your training. Anything that you are disciplined enough to train for, you will master. How well you allow yourself to learn something is what will determine your ability to master it. When you love God, your level of mastery is aligned with His will and He is infinite, so when you don't stop, neither will He.

Potential, if you aspire to become your best in life you must be coachable and you must be teachable. You must be able to be told something and you have to take constructive criticism. To understand anything that God presents to you, you must know that you are under Him and never over Him. An understanding is simply knowing who you are under and your humility is what makes your learning experiences easier. Never lose your focus on learning the importance of listening and never stop developing the ability to accept constructive criticism and sincere teaching.

Good listening skills and humility are two of the greatest qualities to have. They are very ordinary but when you do them extraordinarily, you become extraordinary. You have to listen to live. You can always get better and there is always room for improvement, no matter how good you become at something. The Word of God states that there is nothing new under the sun and there is a time for everything. Part of our job is to make sure we are ready when that time comes and the best way to prepare for your prospering is to practice the fundamentals.

During the latter part of the 1970's until 1990, the Rocky movie sequels were really famous. Revolving around a strong fighter from Philadelphia whose purpose was developed in special ways through the sport of boxing. He trained hard, worked hard, fought hard, and put in the necessary preparation to perform well. Whether it was running the Philadelphia streets, punching meat in a freezer, jumping rope, or running the famous stairs; he put in the work. The fact that Rocky was a great fighter came down to how hard he trained and the time he put in, all in combination with his work ethic, desire, and ability to be coached. In addition to his own work ethic, there was a critical person who contributed greatly to Rocky's success; his trainer, Mickey. Mickey kept Rocky on point and on his toes. He pushed him to be the best he could be through tough love, encouragement, honesty, and passion.

In sports and life it is an extreme blessing to have someone who keeps you sharp, focused and believing in yourself. Someone whose words resonate with you and whose example you appreciate. Aside from holding yourself accountable, it provides a person with a deeper sense of edification when you have someone who keeps you sharp. Constructive criticism can make a world of difference in a person's life. To have someone who can tell you when you are slipping or when you need to tighten-up is a privilege. It is even better when you have someone who encourages you through the criticism and assures you with positivity when you're not on your game. This can elevate you to levels you never knew you could reach.

Most times when you're the one in battle, your view is different from the one who can see the war. You can only see the battle from a fighter's perspective not from a coach's point of view. But when your character is coachable, you develop and learn what you never knew. I've always loved sports because they display the importance of a coach and show how significant connections and relationships between students and teachers can be. One of the main purposes of a coach is to critique constructively to help build a player/person to their prime. When your character is coachable, you can constantly develop into better versions of yourself. Remember, a wise man always works on himself and he constantly makes himself better. When you are reachable, you are teachable and when you are coachable, your character is always under construction because you're always working toward a better you.

Both highly respectable positions in their respective sport, the point guard and the quarterback have core similarities that teach valuable lessons on leadership. Pretty much the commander and chief of their respective fields, they both require knowledge, wisdom, and understanding. Knowledge is knowing how to do something, wisdom is knowing when to do it, and understanding is knowing why you did it. The quarterback position requires you to know how to throw the football, deliver passes accurately, how to read defenses, how to drop back, scramble, step up in the pocket, develop pocket presence, improvise, and more. When you are a quarterback you have to make decisions that instantly affect everyone involved. However, none of those skills are productive if the person playing QB does not know when to use them. For example, a basketball player can have the best shooting form and really have the ability to shoot from long range, but if he continues to shoot in double teams and force shots, that is not using wisdom; however that's relying on knowledge and talent of how to do something, instead of using wisdom and proper discernment of when one should and should not do it. The late Myles Munroe said, "Wisdom protects you from knowledge." Wisdom is the proper application of what you know and understanding is knowing why the time is right.

A quarterback can choose to audible a play because he sees a blitz coming or a cornerback playing up. A guard's responsibility is to facilitate and control the playing field, aka, the court and the same goes for the quarterback. While focusing on being the Point Guard of your life, it is critical to understand your position and your assignment. You have to know your role.

Potential, the most pivotal moment in your life will be when you truly believe that you have potential. That moment is so powerful because your belief is what provokes your purpose and that is what starts igniting your passions. Once your passions are ignited, you become driven and the desire to discover the promises over your life turn into a priority, making your prime the place of peace you never stop pursuing.

For someone pursuing their prime, it is imperative to not only play your position, but know your position so you can do your best to fulfill it. You'll never have to fight for your position if you stay in alignment with your assignment. The point guard is recognized as the floor general and leader because the ball is in their hands the majority of the time. The point guard is also referred to as "the one." At this position, you are expected to pass the ball, make sure your teammates are in the proper place, get them involved, play exceptional defense, communicate, shoot the ball well with consistency, control the pace and rhythm of a basketball game, all while committing as few turnovers as possible. The point guard and quarterback examples can be directly applied to life and the positions that prime seekers learn to master and understand as they grow and mature.

THE POWER OF PRESSURE

P otential chimes in with a question: What's the greatest attribute of a Point Guard and Quarterback? What makes them great?

Consider something Pastor Jamal Bryant said, "Success is when it benefits you, but significance is when it benefits others." Point Guards and Quarterbacks understand that improving their own skills makes them better, but more importantly it benefits those around them. They understand their significance and don't just focus on their individual success. They know that it's bigger than them. They help others see, understand, and develop their potential. Another thing that solidifies who they are is their ability to perform under pressure.

Potential asks, why pressure? What purpose does it serve?

Mr. Prime continues and says well, it's actually the thing that develops "you." Pressure develops potential.

So if pressure develops me, how do I not lose myself at the times when I am under so much pressure? What do I need to do to not lose my cool?

Mr. Prime continues and says, pressure is always proof of purpose. When you are under center and the rush is in your face and the full court press is what you're up against, at that point nothing is more important than composure. To be poised is powerful. Composure is only a representation of the strength of your character, and your character is one of the most important things in life. When you are a quarterback or a point guard, you see and feel the full and first-hand pressure of an attack. It is at times easy to be rattled, but a rattlesnake's rattle is just the warning not the actual attack. When you're rattled, that's your warning sign that it's your time to respond, your time to strike, and your time to perform. The deeper you go, the harder it gets. But the harder it gets, the stronger you become. Always keep your composure.

DAD TOLD ME, POP SHOWED ME

Potential asks, "So what exactly is 'keeping your composure?'" It is understanding the difference between what you can control and what you can't control. That is the definition of 'keeping your composure'. It is how you control yourself in a situation and control yourself while under the many different circumstances that life can present. It is when you lose your composure, that you lose control.

Composure is defined as a self-controlled state of mind. Having control over your thoughts, emotions, and actions are vital because those things allow you to have control over yourself. Once the mind is gone, focus is lost and once focus is lost, your ability to have peace is eliminated. Consider what the prophet Isaiah said long ago, "Thou shall keep him in perfect peace, whose mind is stayed on thee." We are often tested and tests can come at random times, from random people, in random places. We are never totally sure of when we will be tested.

The tutelage we receive and upbringing we receive makes a major difference in our lives, but the application of everything we learn makes the lasting difference. Keeping your composure allows you to think efficiently and effectively while at the same time listening carefully while being able to control and discern your thoughts and actions. Keeping your composure doesn't always control the situation but it keeps you under control and always reminds you of who is in control of every situation.

Something I've learned is the importance of anchoring your emotions. If you aren't rooted then what are you connected to? That means you grow wildly and not wisely. Composure enables you to have control over yourself. Anchor your emotions so you can stand firm, even when the ground is shaky and the waters are rocky. Anchor your emotions so you don't drift so far out that you are no longer able to see your shore. When you lose control, you allow someone else to control you. Nothing should control you except your spirit and your heart, not the ways of the world. Your character is something that will be tested because every day we go through things that try us. Whatever God blesses us with, He will test us with. Self-control and composure go hand in hand.

Your fundamentals are the secrets. If you master those small things, the big things are easier to handle. Even if you never step on a basketball court or play on a football field, still become the point guard of your life and the quarterback of your life. Pay close attention to your surroundings, know your responsibilities and understand what is required of you. Point guards and Quarterbacks thrive not just from individual talent but from the assistance, trust, and chemistry that is built with teammates and coaches. I want you to know and understand that you can never reach your prime quality alone, it takes more than just you. It is the relationships that are formed that give birth to the new levels of potential that exist within you.

A coachable and composed attitude, teachable heart, and humble spirit are all needed for this never ending process of learning. You have to unlearn and relearn, and that requires a lot of humility and patience. Even with all of this being said, it is key to know that you will have some turnovers in life. You will fumble the ball, you will throw some interceptions, you will have some incomplete passes, you will get sacked, you will get plucked, you will be scored on, you will have some injuries, you will have many mishaps, but this is the beauty of what makes you, and determines who you will be. Your mistakes show you what to do better and how to strengthen where you are weak. If you never make mistakes, you will never develop into a better you.

KING OF KINGS

There's a person I know. I know Him well but He is so full of love that I can only continue to know Him better, for as long as I live. The funny part is the more I grow to learn and know Him, He reminds me of how He knows me best. My spirit assures me that He was the greatest to ever walk this earth and He had divine composure and self-control that benefited Him and those He knew. He carried with Him nine different fruits that the spirit within Him produced. His divinity is the very thing that gives purpose to my destiny.

He was the King of Kings, and he had 12 disciples. He was the point guard and quarterback of his ministry and His disciples served as His teammates. Some of them were very devoted and committed not just to Him, but His mission; they were loyal, sacrificial, selfless, and more. Others were disloyal, selfish, dishonest, doubtful, and practiced ways of life that weren't necessarily favorable. However, the King knew that perfection in a person wasn't the promise, but perfection in Him was the purpose. The King has told me before that on this journey of pursuing your prime quality, perfection is not the goal because if perfection is the goal then your faith will have a limit. This is why your greatest self is something you never stop becoming. He shared with me that perfection in Him is the daily goal and the more you believe in His perfection, the more He prospers you into your prime quality.

While having a conversation with one of my coworkers one day, we were talking about the quarterback position and we agreed that when a team has success, the quarterback gets most of the praise, but when a team fails, the quarterback gets most of the shame. The beautiful lesson is, "there is opportunity in chaos." When circumstances are chaotic, you now have the opportunity to display your composure and demonstrate your character. When the King and His disciples were on a ship and the King was sleep downstairs in the boat, there was a very intense storm outside where the waters appeared to have the power to sink the ship and tear it apart. Disciples rushed to the King, "Lord, save us! We are going to drown!" In the midst of the chaos the king replied: "You of little faith, why are you so afraid?" Then He got up and rebuked the winds and the waves, and it was completely calm.

The men were amazed and wondered, "What kind of man is this? Even the winds and the waves obey Him!" With composure and self-control, the King calmed His circumstances and you have the very power to do the same thing. It all starts and finishes with your faith. Your faith is what gives you the confidence to be courageous in all circumstances, no matter how chaotic they are. When everyone looks to you, you have to look to God. The greatest thing a leader can do is follow first. It all goes back to knowing who you are under. The King knew everything, but He still didn't let the things He knew overpower the things He understood. It is sort of an oxymoron, but when you know how to follow, and who to follow, you learn how to lead. Even when you choose to follow, you are being a leader, especially if you are following the right thing or person. You have to first make a choice, and choosing to follow is a grand example of leadership in and of itself.

ZONE IN & ZONE OUT

D on't fall apart because of the pressure, don't crumble. Instead, let the pressure of big plays and big situations stimulate your potential, causing you to perform at your peak. Your prime is discovered under pressure. The deeper you go, the harder it gets. But the harder it gets, the stronger you become. If you are never challenged, you never have to seek new ways to be effective or exercise new tactics and creative strategies that will carry you further into victory. Your greatest achievements mostly come after your greatest adversarial attacks. I must inform you, there will be naysayers, there will be people who criticize, there will be disappointments, there will be people always telling you what you could have, should have, or what they would have done. Even more, there will be doubters, there will be people who do not believe in you, there will be those who just simply hate. This is all a part of becoming your greatest self.

Sometimes leading the pack will be painful but you must persevere through as you push forward. Pressure comes not only from your opposition, but sometimes from those on your side as well. Other opinions will exist. Remember, the field of view is different for a person who lives for others, and lives for something bigger than themselves. Constructive criticism, encouragement, and critiques are good things because they are helping build, however, destructive remarks of discouragement only disassemble trust, and can negatively impact people. It's imperative to be able to distinguish between the two and know the difference.

There comes a point in time where you have to zone in and zone out on what it is that you know works and know to be true. Opposition is an opportunity for you to overcome, never an obstacle meant to overtake you. Your huddle has so much to do with your head, but your heart has everything to do with you getting through.

In order to control any situation you have to compose yourself. No matter how successful you are, or how good you are at something, everyone will not be rooting for you. There will be haters and naysayers, and negative people who don't get intrigued with your success but instead lifted off your failures. This is when you remember what one of the Pillars named James said, "This you know, my beloved brethren but everyone must be quick to hear, slow to speak and slow to anger." When you keep your composure, you will have control over yourself. When you are composed, you can always hear from God. Never let anyone control your emotions in a negative way. In a split second your entire world can change for the better or for the worse, based off of a decision you make.

The truth is, sometimes your storm and hardship isn't even for you. It's to serve as a testimony and example for someone else so they can make it through. Learn to fight through frustration because most of the time your storm truly isn't even for you. You surviving it will help someone else live through it. Do your best to display your faith in your actions and reactions. Sometimes a person's faith and belief is predicated off of your walk. Sometimes you're the only example of God a person can relate to and the only good a person knows. The story of your process is just as powerful as the glory in your testimony. Don't just tell somebody how you do it, show them.

Before Michael Jordan went on to win his six championship rings, he lost to the Detroit Pistons in the eastern conference finals more than once. He may have lost those playoff series, but he never lost his composure. He never lost his confidence, and he never lost his will to win. You cannot lose your will to succeed, you cannot lose your focus, you cannot lose the confidence in yourself, and you cannot lose your faith in God.

HAUNTED BY HUMBLENESS

Potential, I used to have this theory. I used to think that Humbleness haunted me. It wasn't until God gave me real clarity about the word "Humble" that I actually began to understand humility. From the revelations God has given me, I've been able to gather and understand that your gifts will offend some people. Your gift is meant to be unwrapped, not sitting under the tree forever. And when that gift is uncovered or revealed, be unapologetic.

Think about it as fruit. Almost every fruit has to be peeled because the reward is on the inside. There is a revealing and uncovering that has to take place, the skin has to be peeled back. If the outer layer of certain fruits aren't removed then the gift that is inside will eventually rot and become useless. Associate this with your own gifts. Humility doesn't mean hide what you have. It means honor God by utilizing the gifts, talents and special abilities that He gave you. Humility is choosing to use what God gave you. Being humble doesn't mean you always have to eat humble pie because sometimes God wants you to serve it. Arrogance on the other hand is choosing not to use what God gave you.

Your intellect is never above God's understanding. If you'd rather suppress your sanity by expressing nothing, then you are choosing to be weak, not meek. Sometimes your weakness is your silence. Many of us don't know how strong we really are. Muscles are matured when they are worked. You have to exercise your gifts by being bold enough to use them. Use your words and actions to bless, encourage, inspire, motivate, unify, heal, help, save, and love. Speak life as you live.

"That we ought not to think more highly of ourselves than we are but it's imperative to show confidence in what God himself has blessed us with."

—Romans 12:3

True confidence is when you compete with yourself daily to always become better than you were before. Never ever be afraid to be as strong as you are because when things are at their worst, that's when the best can be found in you. Everyone may not be able to play QB on a field, and everyone may not be able to play point guard on the court, but everyone is the leader of their own life. You'll see and understand that the stronger your story and testimony becomes, the bigger your assignments become. More importantly, the greater your life gets, the more humble you should be.

Pastor Jamal Bryant says "In life it's hard to hit high notes and be low key." Don't apologize for shining too bright! How can you apologize for how God has blessed you? You never should. Instead, honor Him by using it for His Glory. Your anointing increases your abilities. Sometimes people apologize for the things they can't do, but we should never apologize for the things we can. Don't apologize because you are great at something. Your gifts will be presents to others so don't be afraid to open them up. This is what elevates you from successful to significant, the fact that you not only benefit from you, but others benefit from you. Use your trials and process to teach. You survived it so you could help someone else get through it. Most of the time your storm isn't even for you, and most of the time your blessings aren't either. Your storms show others how to survive and your blessings come so you can be a blessing. Therefore, let your light shine from the inside out and inspire others by your good example. Allow your actions to amplify your words.

Humility thrives in the "not seen." Humility prepares itself in private, which is why it knows how to perform in public. Humbleness doesn't mind taking the low seat because it knows that it is better to be called up than to be asked to come down. Humility would rather be a quiet man in victory, than a loud man in defeat.

Be encouraged and motivated to succeed in secret first because most of the time private success decreases the chances of being a public failure. Humility is a disposition, a language, a way of living, and a key quality in life. God honors the humble because being humble is always giving Him the glory. Some years ago I heard an echo leap out of the soul of a queen and the message still rings in my spirit today, she told me that a lighthouse does not shine its light for its own purpose. Its existence is substantial, strong, enduring and though beaten and many times alone, it brings others to what they seek; by being a light that never shines on itself. Ultimately, a lighthouse would never fulfill its purpose if it was afraid to shine its light.

So many people have helped me along the way, Potential, so many. I have learned so much from others and learning from them has made me better in ways that words will never explain. Potential, when you have solid support, appreciate it. Be humble enough to know that real help won't hurt you. God helps us through other people so when we have solid support, we should appreciate it. When you are humble you will never be assaulted by arrogance. From a humble spirit springs forth a honest tongue because a honest tongue is matured by a humble spirit. If in humility, you'll make yourself SMALLER, in honor, God will make your life LARGER. –Lance Watson

"For those who exalt themselves will be humbled, and those who humble themselves will be exalted."

—Matthew 23:12

"Humble yourselves before the Lord, and he will lift you up."

—James 4:10

ARTICULATION OF MY IMAGINATION

When you have faith, you must have an imagination. Not necessarily explanations, but simply an imagination. You don't need an explanation for everything when you believe because your imagination knows that it can't fathom everything that God has done, is currently doing, or what He's going to do. An explanation might not match what your spirit has illustrated for you to see. "Eyes have not seen and ears have not heard" that's proof that what He has for you probably won't be revealed to you in the physical. The revelation lies in your imagination. Being introduced to things your mind couldn't fathom, is when you appreciate the spirit. The spirit clarifies what the mind attempts to create. The deeper one taps into their gifts, they see that there is always more wrapping paper that needs to be removed. The top layer serves as the protection, but purpose lies underneath.

Often times we never know how great we are because we don't know how far our impact stretches and who it impacts. And since we don't know, we tend to keep our gift in its wrapper. Whether it be from fear, doubt, or lack of confidence, there are things that lead a person to hide their gift in its wrapper. However, if we understood that we could never collect all of the spiritual stats or see all of the results from our gifts, maybe we would be more confident in using them. The real power of who you are can never be performed if it's put away. If we believed and knew that Glory was the greatest form of our gifts we wouldn't be afraid to be great.

Potential, the definition of greatness is your impact on others. Greatness thrives in the unknowing of its own impact. Often times we never know or believe how great we can be but it doesn't always stop us from doing what we do. When you are good, your greatness eventually grows into Glory. When you keep your eyes on God, He causes the greatness in you to grow into glory for Him.

The gifts God has given you are bigger than you because they are designed to represent Him. Glory is greatness in its most matured form. Greatness revealed is His Glory. God will develop the greatness in you until it glorifies Him.

One of the keys to greatness is making the choice to better yourself every time you don't feel like doing so. When you tell yourself you can always do more and act on that, it's hard to settle.

Always be open to learn and grow and always be broad in your thinking. But never let anyone else's opinion sway your understanding. When you are on divine assignment you don't need an explanation or have to explain to people. As you constantly learn WHO you are in God, you will always grow to understand WHAT to do, WHEN to do it, WHERE to go, and WHY you did it. Your "why" will always match who you are. Your reason never has to answer somebody else's "why."

A few years ago I took a class that changed the intellectual landscape of my life. The teacher of this class, Mr. George London, shared with me that, "There are certain levels. The first level is good. The second level is better. The third level is best. Now if you give what you choose to do your all and do your best, I can't promise you that you will be the best, but I can assure you that you will be one of the best."

Season 4 Summer

THE HOME STRETCH

PACE YOURSELF

Potential is at a place now where it all seems to be happening so fast. The speed of everything is rapid. Acceleration is in the atmosphere. One thing on the heels of the other. His head is spinning because the wind has brought him so much wisdom and he is doing his best to stay rooted.

He sits alone for a while, trying to catch his breath. He starts breathing harder and he even begins to sweat.

Mr. Prime chimes in and says, don't panic…you're only sweating because the seasons have changed. The summer is where you shine, but never forget who you're shining for. Before we embrace the heat, let's make sure we can still hear our hEARts.

Mr. Prime continues…

The best conditioned one, wins. One step at a time, whatever you have to do, just keep moving forward. Your best is up ahead, but you have to move to get there. Living life has its challenges, but in the challenge you'll find out so much more about yourself. Great things take time to develop, even the greatness in you. As you live your life, you constantly learn more about yourself and as I've been on my journey I've talked to myself a lot. I began to just write down thoughts that I felt were applicable to my own life not knowing what type of relevance it could serve in someone else's. Writing became a therapeutic release for me, a place of refuge, and necessity. Constantly opening up my notes in my phone or my document in Microsoft Word and Google Docs to record a thought or idea or even just to vent. It became an everyday thing, everyday something was being added. Something was being contributed to my ideas, goals and dreams. My desires eventually taught me how to trust my dreams.

Frustrating enough, I ran into many moments of discouragement. In addition to trials and life's distractions, I came across thoughts that honestly served as my toughest enemy. Life constantly teaches so many lessons, one being all fights aren't physical. Your weaponry needs adjusting based on the particular arena you are in because your mind engages in more fights than your fist ever will. If you are in a boxing ring you need gloves, if you are on the track you need endurance, if you are a teacher you need patience, if you are in war you need guns and strategy, whatever arena you are in, your artillery must match in order to be successful.

Here's the interesting part though, in some arenas there are more than one enemy, meaning there's more than one type of fight being fought. Your afflictions usually aren't convenient because the adversary doesn't fight fair. You may need many different weapons or simply learn to adjust your weaponry depending on where you are because things could be attacking and challenging you from many different angles, in different places, at different times. For example, if you are building a house and you are using a hammer you may not only need to bang nails in, but also turn the hammer around and use the side to pull a nail out. Sometimes it's just the adjusting of something that leads to the advancement and further development of it. I began to think thoughts about my dream not being the best it could be, will people even believe it, will it impact lives the way I desire it to, will it be misinterpreted, will I even ever finish it…without settling?

In pursuing my prime quality, I saw just how powerful the mind can be, it can either fight for you or against you. When I was encouraged it was as if my mind was wide open and becoming was effortless; but to tell you that this entire process was like that would be more than a lie.

There were days where my mind would be locked completely, nothing could get out. Sometimes weeks would go by without me feeling or seeing progress. I had to understand that pursuing my dream was honestly a great illustration and demonstration of how life is actually lived. Life isn't just flipping pages of a book and going day to day without comprehending anything that you've experienced. Reading a book isn't about skimming over words without comprehending the material. Instead, both processes are about learning and growing. You have to embrace the chapters of your life, understand the context of your seasons, and be able to comprehend your story.

If you were to read your conclusion before your beginning or cross through the finish line without ever starting, you would not feel a true sense of completeness, wholeness, or fulfillment. If God told you that you will win the gold, don't let the 2nd lap make you doubt what He said. Don't let the fluctuations of circumstances change the facts about your faith because your truth is always in your testimony. Don't let pain make you forget the promise and most importantly never forget that you have a purpose. Instead, allow the pain to strengthen your memory by reflecting on what He said and what He has done. A journey is for those who can last, even if they come in last. It's not about rushing to complete it, it's about becoming complete while on it.

I believe that God is concerned more with what we do on our journey versus just trying to complete the journey. Everything has a beginning and an ending but what happens in between is what really matters. Everything that has a purpose has a process that fulfills it. *Your process is the very thing that is fulfilling your purpose.*

Anyone can see the front cover and back cover of your life, but it's when the book is opened and the pages are read, that others can really see the fruit of your life. What you do every day is a reflection of your heart and the type of person you are. Everyday you're alive, understand that you are filling the pages of your book and one day all that will be left is your story, your legacy, and the love that you shared. Play as if it's your last game, love as if it's your last day. You never know when you are in your 4th quarter.

THE ROOT

When God creates something, he doesn't create it for it to stay in its infant form. He creates things so that they can reach their infinite form. A seed is the not the final form, it's only the beginning. You have to see a seed as a tree, and you have to see a tree as a forest. A seed must be cultivated, placed in dirt and experience different elements in order to grow. It has to experience sunshine and rain. Short term goals develop long term thinking, which lead to lifetime achievements. The stronger the foundation, the higher the destination. It all begins at the root.

The roots are where repairs are most important. The height of who you are starts at your roots. Your deepest parts, the things others don't see, the things that are hidden, your very core, the place where the deepest seed can be planted is the depth of your destiny. That depth is your peak because your deepest point is your highest point. When you look at a tree's height, imagine how deep its roots go. As a child, you don't start walking until you have first found balance. A tree doesn't start growing until its roots are strong and secured. If your roots aren't strong, once you reach a certain height you'll just tip over and you'll never see the fullness of what and who you were created to be. Every stage of your life is important. The things you do at ground level, determine the height of the very thing you are building. When there is a problem, you must repair it at the root because when your foundation is weak, your elevation is limited. If your elevation is limited, you'll constantly have the same view because the weakness at your core isn't allowing you to get a peek of higher ground.

If I neglect my weak areas, I will never see the full development of my strengths. Who you are has so much to do with who you were, so if you want to become a better version of yourself, you have to address who you are right now. To recognize self is to acknowledge what is above ground and what's under the surface. Believe it or not the things that are never seen also matter. In the physical a man can't see your next move until it's made but God knows your next move before you figure it out. Man might can't see your preparation but God knows all of your prerequisites. He knows how you prepared for practice before you started practicing, which means He knows exactly how you will perform. Simply put, don't neglect anything about you, nothing. Get to the root of the problem so you can find the height of the solution. Something as simple as acknowledging a problem is a major step. In order to reach your peak you have to first address what is weak and, to go beyond who you were, God has to teach you who you are. Change usually comes before clarity. Once you start doing things a little differently, you start seeing things a bit clearer. Who can go the distance? Don't just be a sprinter, be a distance runner.

ACTIVATED

Don't make excuses. Everything that happens to you in life is meant to make you a stronger example not lengthen your list of excuses. You have the power and ability to achieve all you want to do. Doing it doesn't guarantee success but doing nothing guarantees failure.

If you know what you have to do, then do it. In order to get results you have to take action and have initiative. Make the minor adjustments and trust God to make the major changes because when you really believe, your behavior will change. Realize what you can control and understand what you can't. Sometimes it truly is as simple as just doing your part. Do what you have to do. Stand up, make a change. Change your attitude, your body language…these things will change your performance. Do it before you end up saying you should have done or you could have done or you would have done. Do it so you can say I did it and I did it well and I learned something from doing it.

"Fear is the platform for your greatest accomplishment."- Rosharon Ingram. It puts you in a place where you now have the chance to make the best decision or perform the best action that will ultimately benefit you. It's no need in fearing anything, God did not give us the spirit of fear. "For God hath not given us the spirit of fear; but of power, and of love, and of a sound mind." Therefore take into account that fear is a choice, you have to decide to be scared of something. When you are scared, that is the very moment you make a decision to believe or doubt. When you believe, you have hope and hope leads to faith and confidence, but doubt leads to despair and determent. Doubting deters your mind away from your determination. Doubting gives one a false direction, leading one's mind astray. As soon as you doubt, you have considered failure. But as soon as you believe you have activated faith.

God has instilled in you the power, the love, and a mind that has the ability to withstand and endure any challenge. Your mindset should never be one of defeat and it should never be set in a way where fear outweighs your faith. My grandfather told me when I was young to never ever fear anything, but always pick my battles. This has stuck with me throughout life and it is something I will always remember. Have the courage to make wise decisions about the things you face in life but never fear anything because your faith can defeat everything.

Never ever settle. Always do it for something bigger than you. If you don't believe, start over. Whatever your vision is, see it through completely. Remember, in the fields of faith, seeds of fear never grow. God has so much for you, do your best to fall in love with the process of achieving it all. The wider you allow God to stretch your imagination, the higher He can carry you into Revelation. Respect your process because it fulfills your purpose.

5 P'S

Most of the time, the battle is already won or lost before you even begin. What you did beforehand heavily influences the outcome. There are going to be times when you have to handle certain responsibilities before you can get to the next level, these are called prerequisites. Your prerequisites contribute heavily to the power of your performance, and the pace of your race, because part of your purpose is preparing for it.

Life involves dry seasons. These are times when your seeds aren't producing a harvest at the speed you desire. Nothing may seem to be working out, you don't feel your best, maybe unmotivated, lacking inspiration, or even feel as if your prayer life is dead. A dry season may not produce much on the outside but that dry environment builds up your spiritual cardio. A dry season produces forbearance, teaching one how to stride even when struggling. Your lungs have to be able to handle your current level before they can inhale bigger blessings. The race you are running right now is preparing your lungs for the race you will be running after this one. The bigger the burden, the bigger the blessing and the bigger the breath you can inhale. Your lungs have to be strengthened and able to handle your current level because your endurance is key for your elevation. God wants you to be spiritually hydrated, He wants you to be able to last. Endure where you are, inhale, and take it all in. The higher up you go, the higher the altitude goes and you have to be in shape. A distance runner endures until the end. God constantly exercises your character to keep your anointing in shape.

Sometimes dirt has been dried out for so long it can become as hard as cement with nothing coming out of it and nothing able to go into it. At this stage the dirt is stuck, solid, and almost immovable. The only thing that can help this dry stage is preparation. Preparation, being the changing of climate, environment and actions. Sometimes that may be people, places, or your position, whatever it may be, the bottom line is something has to change. In order for this dirt to absorb, the weather has to be different, it has to be around different air, maybe some humidity or moisture. The ground and foundation has to be prepped. Over time the dirt becomes softer, allowing water, nutrients, and seeds to enter into it. When a surface is hard, it not only prevents things from coming in, but also prevents things from going out. This hard surface can be one's heart, mind, perspective, ability, or attitude. At this point, whatever the hard surface, it will need rain.

It has to be a downpour and one that is steady because the dampness cannot just touch the top of the ground but it has to sink deeply so the water can travel under the surface. When developing your potential, the deepest parts of who you are have to be touched. The teachings you receive in life can't just penetrate your mind but must sink and settle within your soul.

Real comprehension is more than just knowledge for the brain, it is wisdom for the heart and understanding for the spirit. The roots have to be reached. This is what loosens the dirt and prepares the foundation. The downpour of rain, is a flood of pain, a hurricane of hurt, or a tornado of turmoil. The foundation of your heart and spirit have to be prepared because preparation is necessary to reach your promise and your prime.

When I was in fifth grade my teacher's name was Mr. Anton Davis.

Every day he would begin class by making the students recite different poems and quotes and one I never forgot was, "Proper preparation prevents poor performance." I'm grateful for the cadence.

EXPOSED TO EXPAND

After a seed is planted and time passes and the plant sprouts, it is now exposed to many different elements. Elements such as light, oxygen, and people. Exposure contributes to the expansion and elevation of one's purpose. Before you spread your wings, you have to have space to do so. When God enlarges your territory, it is with eternal intention. He knows your wingspan, which is why He expands you. The purpose of exposure is so you can expand. However, it's on you to be open for the opportunities, available for the appointments, prepared for the position, courageous enough for the call, and trustworthy enough to answer. Don't be afraid to think and believe at a different and deeper capacity. When God starts showing you more of your destiny, the dimensions of your vision will change. Expandability of thought will stretch the potential of one's faith and as the potential of your faith matures, the power inside you grows. Once you start believing, it naturally, physically, and spiritually changes things. Your belief becomes the cause of positive effects in your life. The wider God stretches your imagination, the higher He can carries you into revelation. Nothing about God is shallow, therefore, everything about your level of faith should be deep.

Faith is so powerful that even blind faith has vision. Scripture tells you that it walks on its own and not on what it can see. "We walk by faith not by sight." Faith doesn't need sight to get you to the site. All faith needs is itself. So all you have to do is believe. Your faith is a requirement for your planting and prospering.

Nonetheless, once exposed you are now susceptible to the many things your previous stages protected you from. You are no longer underground once you sprout. As God grows and blossoms you, He doesn't make you exempt, He instead shows you the sufficiency of His grace through every area of your life. The more people you meet, the more people you can impact and the more you can be impacted. Your gift may be for the masses and it may not. You can have a great message and just because it doesn't reach the masses doesn't mean its miniature. For example, when a seed for a tree is planted, the person that planted it may not live long enough to see it reach its fullest height but that in no way diminishes the value of that seed. Or from another view, a tree that is deep in the forest of rarely walked grounds may hardly be seen by human eyes but that does not decrease the height of that tree. No matter what, when, or where...if you have purpose, you have power.

Life and its many races are never on a one way street. There will never be a time when every single person is going in the same direction. While you are going east others may be heading west, and while you are going north others may be going south, but in those times of passing, it is when you learn and teach. It is when you see things you've never witnessed, it is when you hear sounds that are new, it is when you begin to get familiar with the foreign.

Exposure is exponential. It multiplies your perspective because you see things from many different views. You can share your experiences to expand someone's mind and they can share their experiences to expand yours. The mind and imagination are truly limitless. You find yourself being able to think on larger scales when you get in the ring with different people, in different places, at different times. Your greatest step is when you step out of your comfort zone because truthfully, you never really know what you are capable of until you are put in a position to perform. When you have the courage to humbly but courageously move is when you encounter God on different levels. Something life has shown me is you can never get ahead of God, you can only meet Him at the spot. "But do not forget this one thing, dear friends: With the Lord a day is like a thousand years, and a thousand years are like a day." 2 Peter 3:8

You will never be two steps ahead of God, even when He accelerates your pace. When you walk in tandem with God, you can catch a stride towards your divine destiny, constantly meeting more of Him, every step of the way. With every stride you begin to take stronger steps towards your purpose. It's critical to remember this, even though you can never get two steps ahead of God, you can get two steps ahead of yourself. This does not mean that you aren't capable but at that moment in time you may not be able. You have the capability but have to develop the ability. You have to crawl before you walk, walk before you run, and run before you stride. Each stage of life has its season and appointed time. The steps of a good man are ordered by the Lord and every step is ordained. Therefore, you should move with purpose and boldness but remember the process at the same time, so you can appreciate your blessings every time. Even when you prosper, never forget the process.

GOLDEN GLOVES

Let me tell you about a giant named Muhammad Ali, who used to be so quick on his feet that he floated like a butterfly and had a sting like a bee. He had a roar like a lion, a soul of gold, and a punch that developed from his potential. He's gone on into eternity now; no more golden gloves, but he is walking on the Golden shores in Paradise.

He used to say that once he retired, he would dedicate the rest of his life to preparing to meet God. Even in that statement, he emphasizes the importance of preparing for something. A lot of times it's not about your skill but your will. As one of the most prolific sports icons to ever live, Ali also said that *"Champions aren't made in gyms. Champions are made from something they have deep inside them-a desire, a dream, a vision. They have to have the skill, and the will. But the will must be stronger than the skill."*

Before we begin any task, we must confront the challenge then have the courage to conquer it. Our greatest self is within. It's that very thing that rest at our core. That seed planted in our soul. The more exposure we get the stronger that seed sprouts; the more that desire develops, the greater we become. In other words, you're a champion before you step into the ring. Once you step into the ring, the manifestation process of who you were created to be, begins. Your preparation leads to manifestation. We all have seeds in us, seeds of Glory, power, love, success, wealth, joy, and more. Don't be afraid to get in the ring and put the gloves on because your training and your trainer will set you apart from the rest. Either you 'gon fight or you 'gon fold, put your gloves on.

REVELATION RELAYS

M r. Prime reaches in a bag that was on the Pier and he pulls out a baton. The baton is made out of gold and has something engraved on it. The engraving reads, "For those who can endure, until the end." Before Mr. Prime hands Potential the baton, he tells him to run this race with patience and remember, the home stretch has two parts. Potential humbly receives the baton as Mr. Prime passes it over to him, but before Mr. Prime let's go, he tells him; your balance and strength is tested on the curve, but your endurance is tested on the straightaway.

Mr. Prime continues…

The reason we must pace ourselves while pursuing our prime is because we are building the endurance of our faith. Every trial is just another session of training. How in shape do you want to be? You can't train the same when your race is different. As you train different, you win different. The stamina needed to endure the faith walk requires training every single day. Your rest is prayer and praise but your grind is centered around Glory. God doesn't operate in time, but everything He does is in the fullness of it. Running the races of life require endurance, not speed. You can't sprint forever. You can only run your fastest for a short period of time, but you can jog and stride for much longer. When you have faith, you can never be late for your fate and you will always be punctual for your purpose. Every blessing that God has for you will be punctual, prospering, promising, purposeful, and perfect. You were born for a divine reason. You were born right here for this season. No one before you could fit in your time or your space, it is only for you. Time is going to be on your side in this season. Your purpose is associated with your pace. It is also associated with your pain because your prosperity is not possible without it. Every finish line is the beginning of a new race and each time you run a new race, do your best to hand the baton off to a better version of yourself.

Pastor Jamal Harrison Bryant said you should "Master maintenance before you accelerate." You have to ask yourself if you are able to maintain your current pace without running out of breath because one's endurance determines their level of excellence. Your training is your testimony. The way you train in private will be revealed in the way you perform in public. Training your spirit in secret makes it a success in public. Practicing is a responsibility. You practice so when it's time to perform, you'll be on point. Failing to train is preparing to fail. The more you train the stronger you get. What used to be a struggle will become slighter. You get sharper, you see things differently. You become swifter.

A lot of people know that you're supposed to prepare for a fight but the special ones know that there is such a thing as preparing for practice. There's a part of you that is ferociously hungry for success and you must find it. Find it, not to become reckless, but to become something you never knew you could be. Succeed in secret first.

"For while bodily training is of some value, godliness is of value in every way, as it holds promise for the present life and also for the life to come." 1 Timothy 4:8.

The quickest way to the finish line is to run for something bigger than yourself.

HIT YOUR STRIDE

When you live, live for your passion. Living for your passion will lead you to fulfilling your purpose. Love what you do. Whatever you do, love it. The thing that gives you that inspiration and inner motivation to work, is the very thing you should probably be walking in. Don't worry about trying to figure it all out, your understanding will come as you move. So move toward that thing with intention, focus, drive, desire, and wholehearted belief. As you put one foot in front of the other, understand that each step is purposeful, even the baby ones. Take your strides believing that every step is carrying you further into the right direction. When you live passionately with affection for the things you do, the only direction you can go is the right direction. Birds fly in the air but if you put a bird in water, it will suffer. Fish swim in water but if you put a fish on land it will suffer. If we attempt to live forcefully and not purposefully, we as people will suffer; ending up in places that don't match our makeup. In other words, living with no discipline and discernment will ultimately lead to destruction. When something is from God, you never have to force it. God teaches us how to grow wisely, not wildly. The desire you have in your heart, will always align with His will when you live for Him. "Passion for the Lord triumphs all logic." It doesn't matter how much you know, what matters is how much you trust in the all-knowing.

Your passionate desire has a clear view of your blessings, don't let fear, doubt, or distractions obstruct your view. Live and let passion be your pace. Your process has to be respected. Respecting your steps is how you develop a stride. You don't drive to your destiny, you are driven to it. This will not always be easy, but remember what your baton says. There will be pain, you will get tired, but endure until the end.

Potential, when you get tired, I want you to always remember that a sign of success is pain and a sign of growth is hurt. Remind yourself that the discovery of pain leads to an understanding of recovery because when you know what hurts, you can appreciate healing. And the more you appreciate healing, the more you embrace it.

Imagine this, as your mantra: the more I hurt, the more I heal, and the more I heal the stronger I get, and the stronger I get, the more I grow, and the more I grow, the more success I experience, and the more success I experience, the greater the Glory of God.

You'll never see the benefits from healing if you've never been hurt. The Glory of God always seems to manifest from grief and pain. You cannot grow and not hurt. However, the pain you feel today will produce peace that you'll have forever. Pain is simply your potential under construction.

God is concerned more with what we do on our journey versus just trying to complete the journey. Everything has a beginning and an end but what happens in between is really what matters. The process is part of the purpose. As you live your life, know that God knew when you would take your first breath and He knows the day you will take your last. Since those two days are determined already and not by us, it gives such greater value to our everyday actions. The life we live in between those two breaths define who we are and how we are remembered.

A basketball game means nothing if nothing happens in between the tip off and final buzzer. A football game means nothing if nothing happens in between kickoff and the final whistle.

What you do every day is a reflection of your heart and the type of person you are. Again, anyone can see the front cover and back cover of your life, but it's when the book is opened and the pages are read, that's when others can really see the fruit of your life. So every day as you live, understand that you are filling the pages of your book and one day all that will be left is your story, your legacy, and the love that you shared.

Play as if it's your last game, love as if it's your last day and be sure to remember the purpose of your vision in every stage of its development. Do not lose sight of it, it's getting closer.

You find your will on the curve but your stride in the straightaway.

Overtime

THE REAL ASCENSION

RUN THE SPADES

M r. Prime takes a minute and just sits with Potential. As they sit in silence, Potential looks over at Mr. Prime as he begins to hear a certain noise. The noise is one that Potential recognizes, but he can't quite determine exactly what it is. It almost sounds like pages being flipped, really fast. As Mr. Prime listens to Potential's description of what he is hearing, he reaches in his bag and pulls out a deck of cards. As he opens the deck of cards, he bends them as if he is breaking them in and he starts shuffling them.

Potential is watching and when he hears the sound of the shuffle, he gets excited and says, "That's it, that's the sound Mr. Prime, that's what I was describing. That's what I was hearing!" Potential smiles, but is a bit confused. He then says to Mr. Prime, "how is that the sound I was hearing, but you just took them out of your bag?" Mr. Prime smiles and says, well, your description of what you were hearing was extremely accurate. You said it sounded like pages being flipped really fast and in fact, that's exactly what it was. You were hearing the pages of your life being turned as they blow in the winds from the world. These cards only present to you an actual demonstration of how that happens. My hands are shuffling these cards and Gods hands, turn the pages of your life. As I shuffle these cards, I never actually know which card will end up where, but the numbers and symbols on the cards never change. The deck of life is already shuffled and the pages of your story have already been written.

While pursuing your Prime Quality, you have to play the hand you're dealt. The pages of your life have already been written and although some chapters are hard to get through, never forget who's the author and finisher of your faith. The dealer and player have a special relationship, just like the author and reader.

Mr. Prime continues, the closer you get to God the more you see how everything He does is intentional. Nothing is "just happening." When trying to get your spirit in shape, your diet has to be the Word and you have to have some believers at your table. While God prepares you for a real stage, He wants you to have a great supporting cast and He will show you your supporting cast by showing you their character.

One of the greatest skills you can have in life, is knowing how to treat people. Your mind is for knowledge but your heart is for understanding. Knowledge is acquired from learning but your heart is the greatest thing that can teach people about who you are. There are some things your heart just gets. We were all created from love, therefore, born to love. Relationships have the power to be one of the greatest resources and rewards in life because to have a real connection with someone is priceless.

Personally, I feel there isn't anything more important in life than relationships. I say that because that's exactly what you must have with God, a relationship. A connection, a bond, something that is built on trust, dependability, and is reliable. It exercises accountability, is helpful, and supportive. Relationships that thrive off love are the ones that always live.

You must nourish relationships throughout your life because they truly do go both ways. No relationship or friendship will last if there is no reciprocity. The more a relationship is nourished, the stronger that bond will grow. Even though, some bonds come and go and are temporary while others are forever; they all serve a purpose. A relationship with God shows you everything you need to know about relationships with people and it's a forever learning process.

You never know what can be developed from a bond, connection, and trust. Could you imagine if a person's salary was based off of how they treated people? If that were ever the case, you would see who is really wealthy and who is really poor. Treating people right should not be difficult because treating people right will never be wrong.

The art of relationships create beautiful and unique stories. The canvas of connections that are created throughout life are always being painted. Your bonds are like visual representations of how your love for others would look if it was illustrated. If you could draw love, trust, respect, and countless other characteristics, the relationships you have with people would be the paint brushes that illustrate those everlasting qualities. How would your picture look?

When I was in college, my brothers and I would always play Spades. It was by far our favorite card game and still is to this day. Spades involves four players but two teams of two on two. While playing this game you develop chemistry with your partner and learn how to win together. I have a tendency to always look at something beyond the surface level and try to discover the message behind it and spades has indeed taught me a lot. Sometimes God will deal you the cards that he knows you play the best. You might not always get the joker, or an Ace, but He knows that the suit He gives you, is tailored for you. Whatever hand you're dealt in life, no one can play it better than you. Always play to win and never underbid your potential.

Spades teaches you how to merge your gifts with another person so you can experience not just individual wins but unified and collective success. It shows you how to develop the gifts in your hand and evolve their potential from solo success to shared significance. The game teaches you how to win together and build from losses. It teaches you how to discuss matters when ideas don't go as planned. It teaches you how to work with what you have. It teaches the importance of always playing to win in life, never thinking for once that your best is not necessary and never thinking that what you have is not good enough. It teaches you how failure doesn't mean fall over and quit but stay in the game and work together with your teammate. The only time you fail is when you don't finish because when you prematurely quit you paralyze the potential of your problem which disrupts it from delivering its purpose. The purpose of a problem is to develop persistence, exercise prayer, fight through pain, mature your potential, and to teach you to persevere. Problems can put us in better positions and actually serve as positives, but it's all based on your perspective. When you have a positive perspective, problems can turn into peace.

Spades shows you the importance of taking smart risks and not making quick decisions that could cost you more than you can afford. It shows you why you shouldn't bite off more than you can chew. The game is symbolic of always having your partner's back, never giving up, understanding the importance of paying attention, maximizing opportunities and thinking long term. One of the most interesting rules about the game is you aren't allowed to see what your partner has in his/her hand until they play a card. You never actually know what is in their hand but you still form a plan to execute.

Not knowing everything is sometimes a really great thing because you exercise your faith and belief on an entirely different level when in the unknown. Your belief determines your next level. If everything was shown to you, you would have no reason to trust. "Faith is the substance of things hoped for, the evidence of things not seen." (Hebrews 11:1)

Being blind to something makes your faith intentional. Your faith has little to do with what you can see but everything to do with what you believe you will see. You have to trust that your circle in life has your back even when you can't see them. Allow your spirit to do the talking, and the listening, as you live.

Anybody can be with you when you're going up but you meet the "real" on your way down. Your road of discovery and recovery introduces you to the real. Maybe that's why the more you recover, the more you discover. Every single thing you lose going down, God has a unique way of restoring in you as He pulls you back up. Your plight only intensifies your purpose and it introduces you to the right people.

Even the things in the way help you on your way. As you reflect on the role of relationships in your life, they will show you how you benefit from environments and how environments benefit from you. Reflective thinking sometimes calls for changes because whenever you truly believe something it will change your behavior. Sometimes those changes are necessary because they create the correct environment for that reflection. In order to reach your inner peace and greatest self you have to sometimes cut yourself away from chaos, which is why your partnerships in life are so important. A real accountability partner doesn't allow certain things to even get near you.

Your surroundings play a pivotal role in your sanity. Your environment has everything to do with your elevation. You can have potential and you can have power, but you find out your purpose when you are in the proper place. The proper place is not just a physical location. Learning how to locate yourself on your mental map while using your spiritual compass as your guide is key. Your heart, your mind, and your spirit all work together as one. When one is out of alignment, you know it. Most slip-ups come from keeping the foot on the gas when we know the oil needs to be changed or the tires need to be rotated or simply when you need some gas. Don't be afraid to go board and bid 4...be smart.

You never know when your strength will be put to the test, which is why training is so important along with your rest. When you prepare, you have to prepare for traffic, make sure a spare is in the trunk, you have a full tank, and other valuables are available. In spades when making your bid with your partner you have to consider possible cuts from the other team and prepare your bid knowing that the unexpected can occur like an accidental cut from your partner. In order to make it to your proper place, you have to be prepared. Don't set yourself up for failure, set yourself up for success. If you set yourself up for success and you fail, it's no doubt that you will come back stronger. But if you set yourself up for failure, you lost before you started. Camaraderie is strengthened in chaos because connections are always challenged in commotion.

You'll never find peace walking someone else's path, but you'll find peace pursuing yours. When you embrace what you have, God will give you more. Your gift always grows when you give it to God. God will show you how to maximize your minimum. Embrace your blessings with love, appreciation, humility, and gratefulness. What you have is better than what you think. "There's no such thing as a life that's better than yours." –J. Cole.

The harder life pulls on you, the harder you pull on God. God does extraordinary things in very ordinary ways, like teaching you about life lessons through a card game. God knows the real you, so be real with Him. Tell God about your process. Don't just tell Him where you're trying to go, talk to Him about where you are right now. The more real you are with God, the better you can love yourself. Your vulnerability with Him will give you a clearer view of yourself.

God loves you in every single stage of who you are. The problem is a lot of us don't love ourselves in every stage of who we are. God loves you even while seeing and knowing the real you. Exposing yourself to Him changes nothing. It only teaches you how to love yourself. If you want to love someone wonderfully, you have to love yourself perfectly; and talk to God honestly.

I long for eternal experiences with permanent people, permanent peace, permanent happiness and everlasting joy. Nourish your relationships and know that connections are worth more than coins. Take risks, but smart risks.

PENNIES & QUARTERS

P otential thinks to himself and reflects on all the meaningful relationships in his life. He is so grateful for everything and everyone he has ever met. He is thankful to know what real value is. He knows that time is precious and he has really built up a lot of courage to continue pursuing his prime quality. He knows he is getting closer, but he also knows there are certain hurdles he has to get over before he gets to the next level. His vision is getting clearer and his call is constantly being confirmed but he has a concern.

Mr. Prime, what about my money?

Mr. Prime responds and says, Potential, your heart is under the microscope of God and all your wealth is within. Wisdom helps one figure out how to withdraw that wealth that is within. Focus on withdrawing some of what has been accruing in you ever since God deposited your destiny in you. I advise you to be interested in the interest. You are not poor, you are wealthy. It just takes a lot wisdom and work to withdraw the wealth that is inside of you. There's an accountant/banker that can help you gain access to that type of wealth. His name is the Holy Spirit. The more time you spend with Him and listening to Him, He shows you how to clean up your credit first. Your credit definitely involves the spiritual, not just the financial.

Put in this context; your brain is a bank account. The goal is to receive knowledgeable deposits throughout life. After accruing funds (knowledge), your bank account (brain) stores some of this knowledge into your savings account (memory). Once your memory has a sufficient amount of knowledge, it then begins to accrue interest (wisdom). The same thing happens with your brain, the more knowledge you receive and store in your mental savings, serves you as a trust fund. However, this acquired fund of knowledge won't just benefit others but always has you as the #1 beneficiary.

Your brain is your safe deposit box. All of the information you learn in life is not supposed to be wasted, splurged, spent on the wrong people, in the wrong places, and at the wrong time. Instead, it should continue to grow, enabling you to do things that everyone may not be able to do, and assist many along the way. You are supposed to enjoy your money, not be a slave to it and you are supposed to always grow in knowledge and never become a slave to your own ego. You want to have discernment with your dollars, be determined with your deposits, and wise with your withdrawals. Anything that the Holy Spirit transfers to you will never lead to an overdraft but always an overflow in your spiritual savings.

Invest in God. Revelations will become your compensation. He will always give you a return on your investments.

"Bring all the tithes into the storehouse,
That there may be food in My house,
And try Me now in this, Says the Lord of hosts,
If I will not open for you the windows of heaven
And pour out for you such blessing
That there will not be room enough to receive it."

—Malachi 3:10 (NKJV)

"For which of you, intending to build a tower,
sitteth not down first, and counteth the cost,
whether he have sufficient to finish it?"

—Luke 14:28 (KJV)

Mr. Prime continues, and tells Potential that most times the outcome of something is heavily influenced before it even begins. He continues and says your plan is important because if you don't plan you have nothing to execute. Before one begins a task, how often does one consider or go through the consequences of a decision whether they be positive or negative? Many times we as people can act fast, without assessing what we are considering. When faced with an assignment, the pre-building stages some would say are more important than the actual building process. Architects have to do countless blueprints, measurements, math, physics, consulting with teams and exercise many more methods of planning before any type of actual physical building is done.

Growing up, there was a saying I used to hear often, "measure 10 times, cut once." The purpose is to spend so much time preparing, analyzing, studying, and planning that when you finally make your move to cut, you trust your preparation so precisely that your performance will be perfect. Bruce Lee said it this way, *"I fear not the man who has practiced 10,000 kicks once, but I fear the man who has practiced one kick 10,000 times."*

If you have the intention to build something, sit down first and add up the cost. Add up the cost to see whether or not you have enough to complete what you are setting out to do. The cost is not always tangible material such as money and resources, but do you have enough heart? Do you have enough desire? Do you have enough grit? Enough discipline? Enough faith? Enough passion? Enough will? Enough patience? Enough confidence? Do you have ENOUGH?

If you never counted up the cost of something but you still purchased it, you never made the choice to see if you could afford what you got yourself into. That is how debt and deficiency is constantly added to our destiny. Affordability is sometimes more important than ability. You may be able to do something but not be capable of maintaining it.

Add up the cost by understanding that there is a difference between your plans and God's purpose for you. Your plans can sometimes divide things up but God's purpose only adds to you. We lose when we start subtracting things that deal with God and adding things that deal with us. When adding up the cost of anything in your life, find out if it's worth it by seeing if God is in it. Ask yourself will your SUM be aligned with the SON? If it's in the SON, it will be in Christ. SUM=SON

The faith walk is not 2+2 or any simple arithmetic, it is an equation from eternity and an equation for elevation. You have to put God and your faith in the blanks. Your search for truth will forever be bland if the pot you stir doesn't have faith as a main ingredient. Your equations may not include numbers so when you are adding up the cost you will have different ingredients being added to your equation, but the sum must always be the SON. It all should point to God, in some way.

After speaking about money, Mr. Prime for the first time in their conversation, gets a little nervous. He sees the sun in the sky taking a different position, which causes certain shadows to appear. Something that has been dark in his life for so long is finally about to be introduced to the light. He is anticipating Potential's next question, fearing that it is what he has battled his entire life. He opens his mouth and says to Potential, never allow the fear you feel, take away your faith in the fight or your fight in the faith.

A 20-YEAR FIGHT
(THE SHADOW MAN)

Potential says I've seen you fight for a long time, Mr. Prime. Your fight has always seemed different. Many never knew of your fight and some forgot about it because it's been so long, but I always saw it. I watched every round, I saw every blow, I saw it. I've always felt connected to you Mr. Prime, so I felt the blows too. I got tired too. I cried with my smile too.

Mr. Prime, can you tell me about it? Tell me about the fight of forbearance.

Mr. Prime doesn't hesitate, he has to answer Potential because he knows his prime depends on it.

He continues...

Growing up with an incarcerated parent is something that is very difficult to articulate, let alone illustrate, especially to those who haven't shared a similar path. This path is one I can relate to because I have spent the majority of my life on it. It's not just growing up and knowing the fact that your parent is in jail and dealing with emptiness and void, it gets a lot deeper than that. I say that because as a person whose testimony was greatly formed from this, I do know what it feels like to have the tables turned and still sit at them. Coming up in an environment where the father is vital, I had that snatched away at the age of two. Gracefully enough, I was blessed with my grandfather who was my main father figure. I'm eternally grateful for him and after his passing in 2012, I do all I can to carry on everything he taught me. However, I've still dealt with the lingering effects and emotions of my dad being behind bars for so long.

I've been a victim of this reality. It's one of those things where time forces you to adapt but you are never really settled with your understanding of it. You sort of just grow to be comfortable in the complacency of the circumstance, but never actually content because the emptiness you feel is the result of the fulfillment you've always longed for. It almost feels like training for a fight and your opponent always forfeits. The steady postponing makes it feel as if a part of your purpose is constantly being pushed behind a wall of prevention and you never get the chance to see if the outcome is victory or defeat. Nonetheless, you still train.

Fresh into my steps as a young toddler, having gloves on my hands that were bigger than me, I was in a ring. The dimensions of the ring stretched a bit further than your normal four corners, and didn't necessarily have a ring girl carrying around the sign to announce the number of the round. Maybe there was some sort of announcement, except these announcements didn't come every three minutes, they came every 365 days. Once a year, the sign was raised and the bell was rung to tell what round of the fight I was in. Never knowing that it would reach 20 years, with multiple rounds through all of those days. A lot of ropes were jumped, countless hours of shadow boxing, sparring sessions, blood, sweat, tears, chicken chasing, role work, haymakers, and more.

In 1993, my dad was sent to federal prison. I have no cognitive recollection of the events that led to his arrest or how everything transpired. My earliest memories of everything were around the age of 3 or 4 when my mom and I would travel to federal penitentiaries. It still amazes me to this day how my mom did this with no maps or GPS, smart phones, or anything similar; even still we always got there. Our furthest journey was to Ohio and Lewisburg, Pennsylvania, but we also visited Upper Marlboro, Maryland, and different parts of Virginia. The furthest location during this time was Kentucky, which was honestly just a bit too far for us to travel by car.

Still a toddler, I can remember my mom telling me that my dad was away at school. This was told to me to protect my feelings or even at that young age show me the importance of going to school and being educated. I'm not sure, but I think I was about 6 years old when I understood that he was actually in jail and not in school. One particular visit I do remember was at Lewisburg federal penitentiary in Pennsylvania. While we were in the large visiting room, there were so many inmates all around with their families, it almost looked like a large cafeteria or multipurpose room. I walked over to the guards table and asked one of the police officers, "Can you let my daddy come home please?" The guards laughed at my innocence and even walked over to my mom and dad to tell them what I had asked, and I still can remember the slight snicker of a laugh my dad always does. Being able to interpret the tone of the laugh at my age now, it was like: "I wish I could come home too, champ, but not yet."

As the years went on and the visits continued, we traveled through snow storms, mountains, rain, and anything else that was on our path. The many different things we endured during these times remind me of the training boxers have to go through. Boxers train in many different environments and have multiple people in their corner when fighting and although many people see a boxer fight, only the closest and most significant people get to see a boxer train.

My mom was indeed significant and beyond special, as she served as the absolute greatest "cut woman" while I was in this fight, because she never let the bond between my dad and I get "cut" off. She made sure the cuts and wounds from this reality never bled enough to blind me from the love my dad had for me.

My dad loved me the best way he could from prison and the only way he knew how. His love language is one that my heart has learned to interpret but often times in my growth left me very frustrated. I've come to the realization of many things about this fight over time that my mom seems to have always knew. She wiped my tears, and consoled my heart, she taught me how to love through hardship and distance. My mom was truly my example of how to love.

In the earlier years of the visits, sometimes my grandfather would tag along. As I grew older, the visits with my mom slowed down some until they ended up coming to a halt for different reasons. I then ended up traveling with my Uncle Phillip who is my dad's youngest brother. We would travel by car as well with my older sister, Arniece, who is three years older than me. I remember my aunt Tammi; uncle Phillip's wife, my paternal grandmother Mildred Hines and my uncle Terrence taking a trip to Ohio to see my dad, around 1997/1998. If I can remember correctly, that was our last visit during that 7-year sentence he was serving. There was an outside part to the visiting room and I remember doing push-ups out there. Thank God for photos because they always freeze the time to show how things used to be and remind you of just how far God's grace stretches.

Moving on from those times, I had reached the age of 9. With many federal prison visits behind me, it had all seemed to lead to a cold winter morning. Snow was everywhere and my mom and I waited in the house. Waiting for something that I was so excited about, I sat looking out the window for hours. My mom, I'm sure having a hard time controlling and measuring my emotions and expectations, just kept her presence near me for that was probably the only thing she felt she needed to do. After hours of waiting and looking, a car finally pulled up in front of my house right on the edge of my driveway. It was him.

My dad and his lawyer arrived, he was just released and his lawyer was his initial contact person due to legal actions and things with the halfway house. Filled with excitement and nervousness, that cold day had all of a sudden become warm as I sat on his lap in the living room.

For about 2 ½-3 short years, I had access to my father in the physical when he wasn't in jail. I remember a trip where we went to Kings Dominion, him coming to see my championship basketball game at Stephen Decatur Recreation Center, riding with him to Tysons Corner mall, along with a couple other memories. Life was pretty cool for those few short years. I was still in elementary school and was just a kid who knew his dad was home. Living in Clinton, MD for the majority of my life, I attended James Ryder Randall Elementary school and I remember him coming to the school one day when I was in 4th grade just to talk at the table in the main lobby. He had on a pair of timberland boots (some butters), a sweatshirt, some jeans and a winter hat. He attended my back to school night that year as well. During this time we never lived together, but I remember him coming over the house for a few, just to stop through. I remember us first going to the barbershop together when he got home, him going to sign me up for football, spending a couple nights at his apartment with him...I just remember.

He had brought me a basketball goal that year for Christmas and a dirt bike some months later. I remember my grandfather letting him drive his conversion van to North Carolina that summer for a family reunion. Even on that trip, I remember being in the hotel room waiting for him to come back up from playing cards. It was fun being with my dad for those years. It was a balanced combination of longings, aspirations, questions, love, and hope all evenly dispersed in the same pot. His presence temporarily filled the voids but the uncertainty held the truth in a place where it was never understood. With vague but vivid memories of those three years, it isn't until talking to you now that I recognize how those years were foreshadows of what was coming. Those years were fast; and even with glimpses of hope, happiness, and light, for some reason shades of confusion, incompleteness, and darkness still existed.

"He that dwelleth in the secret place of the most High shall abide under the shadow of the Almighty."

—Psalm 91 (KJV)

When I think about a shadow, I think of a dark shade or visual outline of something or someone. It's something that follows a person. With every step you take, your shadow is always with you. However, the shadow is only visible when a body is between a ray of light and a surface. In boxing, shadow boxing is a training technique used to teach the fighter how to anticipate and act as if he is actually fighting someone, but there is actually no one in front of them. This technique prepares the boxer for the real opponent.

During the summer prior to starting fifth grade, I was outside playing basketball and I came in to get some water. As I came in my mom called me down to her bedroom. My dad was on the phone. When she handed me the phone, I was hit with unexpected and unbelievable words…"I'm in jail man." I honestly couldn't believe it, but was too young to register it fully. All I remember thinking is, "Again?" Throughout my life, I've always sort of felt like this entire situation was a shadow that followed me. For 20 plus years I've had to fight something that I could never actually hit, like the shadow boxer. However, unlike shadow boxing, I could always feel the hits.

In spite of the black eyes and busted lips from this fight, I embraced it all because I love my dad. He has been someone I've always celebrated. He is a star to me. I never knew exactly what he did but it didn't matter to me, I just knew he was my dad and I loved him unconditionally. However, as time fast forwarded and I got older, his absence not only affected my early childhood days but my young adult years as well. For years I've been the son who never told his dad no. Saying no in general was always something difficult for me to do, I've always tried to do what I could for people even if my heart was saying no. When my dad asked or needed anything I would do everything in my power to help him. Phone calls, running errands, locating lawyers, handling business, going to take care of other siblings, etc. This is a lot more hectic than it may seem, but picture a kid whose dad has been locked up for his entire life. Once the kid finally reaches a certain age, the dad figures the child is mature enough to handle certain things and starts asking him for favors. At 25, I still haven't had that one-on-one visit with my dad that I have longed for, for so many years. I share all of this because I intend for my hurt to help.

Sometimes talking to my father was aggravating, it seemed as if he would call me 100 times a day, every day. Every time I looked up, he would be calling my phone, every half an hour, calling me. If I missed the call then he would call again, back to back until I was able to answer. When I answered he would say what's going on with the phone, in a tone that seemed to be completely oblivious to anyone else's feelings. This grew to really frustrate me because it was like the quantity of phone calls was through the roof, but the quality of conversation was in the basement. We weren't talking about much, I was only handling things he wanted me to handle and he would only call back to make sure that things were handled. Whether it be sending him money through Western Union, making phone calls, trying to contact people, whatever it was. There were literally days when he would pretty much dictate the outcome and schedule of my day before he had even spoke to me. He would call me, and start assigning things for me to do; run here, run there, call this person, call that person. This was nerve wrecking and what I considered to be very selfish and even inconsiderate at times. It was almost as if he didn't realize that I was a young adult who had his own life, own plans, own thoughts, own responsibilities, and who had grown up and gotten older. Or more importantly, just a young man who wanted to talk to his dad or be asked "How was your day?" Calls would start as early as 6:30 in the morning sometimes and go all day until about 8:45 at night because the prison would lock in at 9:00. The once wisdom filled conversations that I longed for and appreciated so much had turned into just straight up check-in sessions.

Frustrating, irritating, and even annoying. These adjectives may be harsh, but this was ongoing for almost two years. Can you imagine not having him physically here but having that longing and grief almost shift to a form of resentment? When the prison would go on lockdown, I would honestly take a deep breath and say "man, ok now you can get a moment to yourself, a few days, maybe a week. I didn't have to check my phone by the half hour, or be on a schedule all day long. If I missed the call, I wouldn't have to hear about it later. I don't want anything to be misunderstood, I love my dad, more than he knows because I've never had the opportunity to even tell him fully or let my life show him. But if I tell you about my fight, I have to tell you about each round, even the ugly ones.

It was no longer about, "man, I miss my dad," but it grew to a point where it was, "man, let me be my own man," respectfully. You can't control things from a prison, and when you try to do so, it affects those that love you the most. It's been so much built up emotion, you can say that P's & Q's during these years translated to Pain & Quiet. I think pain is one of those things that is so easy to disguise, but so hard to describe. However, I've definitely learned that pain produces a heavier dosage of your purpose.

The patterns my dad displayed intensified. It translated to him even having an attitude and asking me questions like "man is it something you want to tell me?" Little did he know, it wasn't even anything like that, but if I haven't talked to you in two weeks because you've been on lockdown and the first thing you say to me after those two weeks is "ay do me a favor and take this here", I think that would affect any child. Being the child of someone who is incarcerated can actually sometimes have you feeling as if you inherit their problems, their shortcomings, and even some of their history. It can make you feel like you're actually the one in prison, but without the physical bars. Instead, trapped and in bondage, psychologically. You pretty much feel emotionally incarcerated never knowing when your release date is for peace of mind.

I never really went into deep detail with my mom about any of the things I felt in regard to this situation. I never wanted her to stress over it or become sad because of it because the truth is she already was. She hugged me one day and told me that she felt so bad and was sad because she has never known what it is that I've felt. She said I just don't know what it is that you have felt or that you feel and I'm so sorry. These thoughts have been deeply internalized, not necessarily by choice, but just because the depth is so deep. I questioned who would even have the time to listen to me pour out random facts and events that happened in my life when it came to growing up as a child with an incarcerated father and a kid who had a hard time expressing the "inexpressible."

I want you to understand Potential, that when you internalize things, you can potentially paralyze parts of who you are. You can potentially paralyze your prime. You have to heal to become your best you.

Potential listens to all of this and is nervous about what will happen to Mr. Prime as he is opening up his heart and making it susceptible to everything in the world. He realizes that Mr. Prime is transforming because of his transparency and Potential is stunned because he remembers what he prayed for before he ever spoke to Mr. Prime. He prayed that his transparency transformed him and now for him to witness that happening in Mr. Prime is giving him a sense of hope, but he still has questions. He thinks about the things that were just said to him and he opens his mouth with another question, "But what if the pain has a lock on my heart that forces me to keep it all in?"

Mr. Prime says, if you keep it all in, you'll never be clean. You have the power to unlock every part of your purpose that has been locked away by pain. Sometimes the key could be crying because crying is just releasing, and when you cry you cleanse. At some point in time, you have to open up.

Always remember, growth comes from grief, so your tears basically water the soil of your soul. Your tears water the parts of your purpose that have experienced droughts. The heart sometimes needs to shed itself so it can stay on beat, and when the heart is on beat, the soul learns how to sing its song. Plus, when you open it up and release it all to God, the more He can get in and release you.

Mr. Prime continues...

I know that my dad has been in jail for the majority of my life and I know that he has missed a lot of things. I know that he pretty much missed my entire childhood, and I know that he's thought of this and handles it in his own way. I have never condemned my dad, judged him, or turned my back on him. In fact, I sympathize with him so much that I often and pretty much always allow my compassion to just lead me to put myself and feelings last. I know the list of people he could depend on was not long and in fact I probably am number one on the list, however, time has given me the opportunity to truly hear from God about this.

God showed me through time that I had to have a stronger allegiance to Him than to any one else in life. He also showed me that I wasn't the only one fighting; my dad was fighting too. We had the same opponent but were fighting it in different places, attacking it from different angles and the result sometimes was us hitting one another. We were fighting something that could see us, but we couldn't see it. The darkness of the shadow tried to dim the rays of hope but as the Word of God says, a longing fulfilled is a tree of life. This fight was helping me reach my prime quality and helping my dad reach his too.

Consider the Psalmist, his name was David. He once said that "He who dwells in the secret place of the Most High shall abide under the shadow of the Almighty." During this fight, God told me to keep going further into those secret places. When you seek God like that, wherever you go, you will be in His shadow. There's nowhere He can't go because He's already everywhere. Everywhere you go, God will already be there and not only is He already there, but He is with you every step of the way as you make your way further into Him. God showed me that when you seek Him in the secret place, He will start telling you secrets. And to know God's secrets is the secret to reaching your prime quality. Think about what He says when He says "under the shadow of the almighty." A shadow is always with you, but it's only seen where there is light. If you remember this during your fight, you won't be able to get away from God because you'll be under His shadow and it's from His shadow that He carries you further into the light. The secret place is where He shows you the purpose of privacy and why training in private is so pivotal for you, Potential. Sometimes what He has to say to you is so heavy that He wants to tell you in the dark first. Never forget, the seed grows in the dark.

Everything you're about to grow into is going to be so incredible. You will only grow further into the light because you abide in His shadow. To be under the wing of God is to see life from the secret place. To be carried places you could never dream about. Places you could never ask to see because you could never think, dream, hope, or even imagine them. God is going to start telling you some things in the dark only to brighten the light in you. Remember, everywhere you go, He's already there. His word is the lamp at your feet and the light to your path.

A 20-YEAR FIGHT
(CUT THE CUFFS)

Being a child of an incarcerated parent for my entire life, I had the unfortunate privilege of living this life but I had to understand that this too fell under the umbrella of Romans 8:28: "All things work together for the good of those that love God and are called according to His purpose." To have lived a life that gets to experience the effects of this plague is something so dangerous to one's potential but it has the power to push a person further into their promise. The pain from this gave me a powerful perspective about prison.

My dad's fight took place inside. He wasn't just locked up, but locked away. He had a limited boundary placed on his ability, capability, and reality. His potential was halted, limiting what he could do in the physical. In prison, you cannot travel or move at your own pace, it's almost like a time capsule that keeps you in a stage but you age while in the stage. You physically get older but what you see in the physical is not changing. For example, hearing my father talk about being in one place gives me the perfect example. He told me, when he was moved from one prison to the next, he saw a car, for the first time in almost 10 years. Every day he could only see the sky, but no roads. I guess the symbolism is you can never see where you're headed, but the sky constantly reassures you that there is more out there.

Prison paints a picture of the ultimate low seat. Imagine being in a large lecture hall constantly being reminded of the same lessons that you were presented before you entered this world of bondage. There are countless textbooks consisting of chapters that are relevant to what you know and see but how can you turn the pages to a bigger tomorrow if your physical eye only sees the same classmates/inmates, classrooms/cells, and memories. There is no physical expansion but a constant repeat of your yesterdays. Your days begin a bit earlier and they end a bit earlier….it's almost as if you never get to see your later development because you are locked in a certain hour and everything is controlled and measured. You have boundaries on your time, boundaries on your space, and boundaries on your ability to comprehend the advancements of society. Prison offers one of the greatest paradoxes, it's almost like you can be a veteran but a rookie at the same time. You have mastered the art of commissary but you are learning how to color the outside world while staying in the lines. You have images but everything is black and white. You are preserved but are you rehabilitated? Regardless of how one interprets prison, I think we all agree on one thing, your physical access is limited. Your faith is truly tested because you have to make a conscious decision to believe that you are growing even when you can't see it and that your freedom is connected to your faith and not your physical.

Mass incarceration is something that has left people and families distressed, damaged, and in detrimental conditions. I keep saying "physical" because physical circumstances and conditions can distract the mind and real defeat only happens when the mind is destroyed. Once an inmate reaches a "mental" shutdown, then all of the physical limitations travel to the mind which leads to the heart accepting hopelessness. Some examples are suicide, violence, and depression, and these are the dangers. Your mind is your gateway to manifestation, your heart is your highway to heaven, but incarceration is the infection and prison is the plague. It is a disease that immediately attacks the mind putting one's potential in great danger.

Realizing that my perspective may not be 100% correct, it has expanded my purpose 1000%. I had to realize just how big this fight really was. This fight wasn't just 20 years on my end, but 20 years on my dad's end too.

While the effects from this prison plague are deadly, freedom is also associated with this theory. It may not make much sense because freedom is the opposite of incarceration, but this is just what God has shown me. When isolated the mind can reach measures it never knew it was capable of reaching. I believe that when the flesh is locked up, it's then that the spirit is released. Flesh being physical and spirit being spiritual mind, heart, and soul. Spiritual revelations come from fleshly incarcerations. The Word of God tells us that we have to die daily. Our flesh has to die because our flesh shutting down allows the spiritual gateways to open up. Rakim, considered to be one of the greatest rappers of all time, has a lyric where he says "if I get sloppy in sin, then the prophecy ends." Essentially meaning if I allow my downfalls, flaws, vices, and errors to take hold of me and blur my spirit, then I will never be able to reach the destination because I'll be caught up in incarceration.

This pain has taught me that prisons are not just penitentiaries. Prison can be your mind, your heart, your views, and more. It is when your lights are shut off. It is when you are a slave to yourself. However, the truth of the matter is this, it is when you are locked away that you can be unlocked by God. He is the locksmith to all of your prisons. That type of freedom starts from within, and your joy does as well. Liberation is for your celebration. You find your freedom in your faith.

A 20-YEAR FIGHT
(MY CORNER)

I've learned so many incredible lessons from my dad, but I often ask myself if I would have learned those lessons from him if he weren't in jail. I know that the Lord's plans are perfect and His will is flawless, so even with the misfortune of having my dad spend the majority of my life in jail, I've come to understand and realize that I may not have the relationship I have with him; had he been home. On a long list of things I've learned from my dad, the three major lessons I've learned are never stop fighting, always keep your composure and understand what can happen when you aren't on your P's & Q's. Life has shown me how easy it is to get in trouble when you are doing the right thing, so just imagine how easy it is when you are doing wrong.

When I was a sophomore in college my dad told me that they were having a trivia contest at the prison during recreation. A lot of the inmates were in the rec area and the contest involved a question, whoever came up with the correct answer would receive free commissary for a specific amount of time. The question was: "How many seconds are in a day?" He said he immediately knew that he could figure this out but the catch was the inmates could not use any pencil or paper. He said after doing the math in his head for a few minutes, he raised his hand and said 86,400 seconds. Other inmates looked on like "how in the world did you get that in your head", the guards responded "that's correct Hines" and granted him his free commissary. I was amazed by his ability to figure that out but even more awestruck by the message behind it.

My dad told me that there are 86,400 seconds in one day and that shows you how much time there is for you to do the wrong thing and get in trouble. As a black man, you come into this life with two strikes already, you are black and you are a male. One mistake can literally ruin your life. You have one strike to earn before you are in the system forever. The fine line lies between how you use those 86,400 seconds.

Your P's & Q's are so important because all it takes is one time to "take away your time." My dad has always told me to pay close attention to my surroundings, stay around positive people, positive places, and around positive potential. He told me to flood my schedule with so much positivity that it leaves no room for negativity. There's a lot of time in one day. Every day matters and every second is critical.

This 20 year fight has amplified the meaning of P's & Q's. Everything happens with purpose and my father's incarceration with as much pain and confusion that it has given me, it has given me even more clarity and peace. It tells me how critical it is to do the right things and do your best to stay on the straight and narrow. My dad's example has been grand for many reasons. He serves as an example of what can happen when not on your P's & Q's but he serves as an even stronger example of God's grace and how being on your P's & Q's helps you survive the toughest consequences. My dad and I had to learn how to fight in the dark. It is in fact this fight that has made our connection that much stronger. My dad has shown me how to stand under some of the heaviest burdens, but at the same time, knowing in your heart that God will never put more on you than you can handle. Further emphasizing the point that, the weight you feel is only the weight of glory that he is waiting to release in your life. I think this is a fine time to tell you that going 100% for God does not mean you won't mess up. However, He shows and tells you how to clean up what you messed up.

Everything we ever need we are born with, but it's the life we live and the experiences we have that help us tap into the unknown power and potential we possess. The experiences we have help develop what is already inside of us and help us discover more of our deeper selves. Specific encounters may enable a person to think differently which can increase their desire for deeper human knowledge and understanding. Encounters can also spark hope and faith. Different levels of circumstances create different levels of courage.

Mr. Tony Lewis, Jr. wrote a phenomenal book entitled *Slugg-A Boy's Life in the Age of Mass Incarceration*. In this book Mr. Lewis gave the most authentic narration of his life and the things he experienced growing up with a dad who was super successful in the drug game until his fall. When Tony Lewis, Jr. was nine years old, his father was sent to federal prison. He mentions the deepest and darkest places that he had to live and survive through; his friends dying, his family members dying and going to jail, his mom suffering from mental illness, living through poverty, surviving shootouts, and crap games, just to name a few. This man and his testimony was so raw and real that it was honestly one of the best pieces I've read. The rawness is what made it so real. He did exactly what my dad always told me to do, he turned every negative into a positive. His service and role in his community and society serves as proof.

In heavy anticipation for Tony Lewis, Jr.'s book, I had been following him and his work on Social Media since 2011. He caught my attention because of the work he did for DC and its urban communities along with the work he does for returning citizens, making their transition back into society the best it can be. He also created a brand called #SonsOfLife. Sons of Life was an initiative he started for children whose parent/parents were doing life in prison or a long sentence like his pop. After seeing this, I said to myself that this was something I could relate to 100%. I knew of this pain, I could talk about it, listen to people's stories, all while having my own story to tell. I wasn't alone.

I knew the things I had experienced, and although they were nowhere near the things Tony Lewis, Jr. experienced, I was a soldier on a different battle field, with a different type of armor and artillery. I was fighting a battle that required other essential weaponry that wasn't steel or clips. It was the armor of God that I needed. A wardrobe of Glory.

I needed a sound mind, a strong conscience, a listening ear and discerning judgment. I needed humility, manners, respect, and a strong character that was resilient and stood firm. I needed something called a belt of truth and a breastplate of righteousness, my feet ready in the gospel of peace, a shield of faith, a helmet of salvation, and the sword of the spirit. I needed to pray in the spirit. I needed faith. I needed to believe in myself. I needed to be a kid who didn't live life like a gangster or hustler, unless I was hustlin for God.

My mother kept me involved in absolutely everything positive. There was a time where I played on three basketball teams at once, AAU, at the local rec center, and my school team. I was active, always playing basketball. I was in countless camps; the Dream Makers Academy; then known as the Run n Shoot in Forestville, Maryland ran by Coach Willie Diggs who was amazing by the way. I went to University of Maryland Basketball camps when I was a child, back when UMD won the National Championship, when Juan Dixon, Steve Blake, Lonnie Baxter and Gary Williams were there. Basketball was my life at a young age and I have to thank my mother for that because she was doing this as a single mom.

My mom was not yet married and my father was locked up, I can barely remember phone convos with him back then. And of course my mom and I had the support and push from my grandfather and grandmother. I was fortunate and very, very blessed.

My point is I was always active and my mother and grandfather were the catalyst to it. The support I had was incredible and it wasn't until I grew older and more keen of others to understand just how blessed I was. My appreciation is on another level now than it was when I was a teenager. Not to say that I didn't appreciate it back then but the more you grow, the more you know. In saying all of this, my biological father was not here. This is why I admire, appreciate, and will forever remember my grandfather and the things he did for me because it was him who filled the father shoes and was my dad for the 21 years.

My support system has blessed me, immeasurably. There is in fact a moment in my life that I will always remember and it involved three men; my grandfather, my dad, and my stepfather. When I was 13 years old, my grandfather and stepfather drove me to see my dad in Hazelton Federal Prison. My stepfather not only stepped into my life, but he stepped up in my life, and stayed in my life.

I saw three men come together selflessly, all for me. We all sat in the visiting room and talked. I saw them converse, connect, and show their immense love for me through conversation. What many would consider off limits territory because of false societal norms regarding relationships between biological fathers and stepfathers, my dad and stepdad reversed that curse and showed me otherwise. They showed me something I had never seen before; my dad displayed humility and maturity in one of its purest forms as he embraced, appreciated, and respected my stepfather. My stepfather did something many have never done. He not only was there for me but he took me to see my dad, in prison, and sought no recognition for doing so. He did it because he loved me and honored my father and his role in my life; even in his absence. I've grown to appreciate that moment more and more because it was an example of love that was so peculiar. The most powerful moment during the visit happened when we were leaving. As we all approached the exits, after hugging my dad I glanced over at him one more time and I saw him looking at my stepfather. The look on his face matched the words that came out of his mouth, "Ant, thank you man." In the midst of reflecting on all of this, I see how my stepdad and grandfather helped both my dad and I with our fights.

Although Tony Lewis, Jr., and I may have had a difference in environments where we were raised, we did have something huge in common; an incarcerated father. There was one place we both knew very well and that was the Federal Bureau of Prison's visiting room. We knew the "this is a collect call from" or the "this is a call from a federal prison" "Press 5 to accept." We knew the Western Union transactions or putting the phone down or running here and running there. I too had pictures of myself while sitting on the lap of Rayful Edmonds (one of the most infamous drug lords of the 21st century). I too took long road trips with just my mother as we traveled to Lewisburg, or Ohio to visit my father. I too had been to the prison in Lorton, Virginia. I too knew about crying in visiting rooms or holding back tears, and just having so many questions. I too knew what it was like to talk through the glass while using the phone, or having to bring a lot of change in quarters so you could buy stuff out of the vending machine during the visit. I had lived that life, not the street life but the child of the incarcerated life. I felt the effects from the past and the prison pipeline. "I ain't slang in the 80's but, I feel the pain y'all went through" (-Wale).

As I read through Tony Lewis, Jr.'s book I saw more and more that I could relate to. On July 31, 2015, I had the honor and pleasure to meet Tony Lewis, Jr., at Bus Boys & Poets on 5th Street, NW, DC at his initial book signing. As I approached him I shook his hand and I said, "Sir I'm glad I can finally meet you and I too can relate to #SonsOfLife. My father has been incarcerated my entire life." He looked up at me immediately with piercing eyes as if he instantly knew and said with a slight smirk on his face "Oh yea? Well, this is for us." I appreciated that moment because it brought me assurance and clarity to know that even though I felt for so long that no one could relate nor understand, it was Tony Lewis and his story that strengthened my entire perspective and broadened it entirely. His book provided me with a peace. I always strived to live right and do what my parents told me, and to stay on my P's & Q's. Honestly meeting Mr. Lewis was a reward and reading his book was a blessing.

Having a talk with my mom one night, we shared and talked about the feelings I was experiencing when it came to my father sparked by my frustration and internalized feelings. My mom always gives me her ear and her heart. Just us, sitting in the basement of our house, she let me release. Just pour out thoughts, emotions, frustrations, and compressed sentiments that have never really been dug up. My phone was upstairs in my room, no distractions, no TV, just us talking. Her laying on the couch wrapped in some blankets and me sitting in the chair with my feet up. The relaxation that surrounded the talk was amazing. As we talked, our conversation centered on my frustrations with my father.

I often say that when I am speaking, I find it difficult to accurately express what it is exactly I am feeling. My mind moving faster than my lips maybe, or my lips moving faster than my heart, or somewhere in between. Nonetheless, on this night, the rush of feelings seemed to boil over with nothing but space to splash on to. My mom gave me space, opportunity, and time to deliver long lost packages of pain. During this discussion, as I put so much out, it seemed as if, in me pouring out, I started to be poured into. (As I emptied my cup, God started feeling me back up).

Sometimes the only way to experience relief, is to release. Often during the convo my mom would say "son don't get angry, love on you, let your heart live, she told me everything is going to be ok and to remember every single thing my grandfather taught me." She told me "it's already been laid out for me, so why not eat?" In other words, "Craig, you spend so much time preparing food for others and serving that you forget to eat."

Although service is great and one of the keys to ministry, my mom wanted me to understand that I can't take care of anyone else unless I take care of myself. How can I hold others up and help others stand if I'm falling down and too weak to stand on my own? I can't be a crutch if I'm on crutches or better yet I can't be a crutch if I'm crippled.

Your sprain may lead to a strain, your fracture may lead to a break, your break may lead to a breakdown. I can't charge others if my battery is dead. I can't serve if I am starved. I have to love my imperfect self perfectly so I can love others correctly and completely.

My mom always gives me something of great meaning, I honestly think sometimes she doesn't even know the value or power behind her words. I always tell her, it's nothing like a mom's approval. So during our convo, I was thinking and the thing I thought of was "The Art of Expression." Around this time is when I slowly began to start seeing the importance of truly releasing. The Bible tells us to not pour new wine into old wine skins. So I shouldn't associate and try to blend old pains with new promises. Basically, what happened is not bigger than what will happen, therefore, I should not size up my present based off the size of my past. God never puts our best behind us.

The old cannot contain the new, so I have to understand that sometimes you grow too big for your cage. Your cage cannot contain your call because your destiny is bigger than your defeats. Your destiny is bigger than your disappointments. Your destiny is bigger than your deferments. Your cage cannot keep you from reaching your calling. When you get too big for the cage, you have to get out. You have to leave and grow as big as you are meant to be, not as big as your circumstances are allowing you to be. There are many things that can help one realize that their cage is now too small for them. Some break out of their cage viciously, some pry it open with wisdom, some are released, some pray their way out, some shout their way out, and some express their way out. I'd like to place myself in the pray and express category. On this night of talking with my mom, I realized the ability to express yourself fully, is a gift that some will never be able to unwrap. However, when I learn to express what lies deep, I can then jog on the shores of understanding. In that moment, Mr. Prime says, "walk with me down to the shore real quick." Potential responds, "What shore?" Mr. Prime says, "Just come on, trust me, it's the most beautiful thing ever."

THE GOD SMILE

A s their stride carries them to this place, Mr. Prime sings a song from a Queen named Helen Folasade Adu. He says that she contributed to his understanding of his prime because she taught him that it was never a crime to cherish the day. Encapsulated by the aura of the atmosphere, he sings her lyrics, "Help them to strive, help them to move on, help them to have some future, help them to live long, help them to live life, help them to smile." While singing, he hears the wind as it calms, because even it understands the power of one's prime quality. As the silence reaches its golden sound, Mr. Prime stops as well to hear the perfection of Potential's purpose.

Stunned at what he sees, Potential sits in awe. His soul is singing a different song and his heart knows the cadence of the beat so well as if it's a part of his promise. The lyrics seem to answer the questions that he was about to ask Mr. Prime. He starts to hum what he hears his soul singing and he says to Mr. Prime, how did you find this place?

Mr. Prime responds and says, well I wouldn't say I found it, I'd say it found me. It found me when it was hard to smile, it gave meaning to the many emotions I've felt throughout my life. It applied an illustration to some of the most beautiful things my imagination has ever fathomed. It taught me that God's Smile is the light that shines on you and the light that shines in you, and that light taught me about illumination. It taught me how to illuminate by faith.

Potential says, I get it, I get it. I remember before you said that sometimes things have to find you. I get it, but how did you know this was here? How did you know that it would look like this, right now at this very moment? How did you find this place, how did you know this even existed? Tell me Mr. Prime, tell me how you found your way here.

Mr. Prime smiles and as he smiles, the brightness of his smile illuminates what is within and he softly says...my grandfather always told me I'd find my way through the city.

They stare out into the smile of God and he continues...

Pain teaches you how to smile. Pain always makes the smile stronger and grief always makes the glory greater. Your smile is the enemies' trial and your celebration is his tribulation.

I want you to understand this. God does the unthinkable. Specializes in the impossible. Has a Master's in the unusual and a PhD in the incomprehensible. He created the curriculum of life. He's the Professor of your purpose. The Dean of your destiny. The Principal of your passion. The Teacher of your testimony.

Let me tell you about something that happened to me on August 3, 2016.

It's amazing how God can use anything to communicate something to you. With Him, everything is purposeful and nothing is purposeless. On the morning of August 3, 2016, I got my wisdom teeth pulled, all four of them. The pain I experienced that day has far exceeded anything I could have imagined. Everyone's experience with the procedure is different, however mine's unfortunately was horrible. The night before the procedure, I was tweeting about tears and their symbolism, not knowing that the next day I would cry from pain. Once the anesthesia wore off, it was so intense that I was shaking in my room. So frustrated from what I was feeling, I just wanted relief. Along with the normal recovery routine for a procedure like this, I hadn't imagined it being this bad and I was already expecting the worse. Arriving at the oral surgeon that morning, getting a final X-ray before going in the room, the doctor told me the walls would turn into waves. I guess that was his way of telling me I was about to fall asleep because of the anesthesia. After feeling it injected into the I.V., I laid there with a few thoughts. Thoughts of my grandfather, I prayed, I was really nervous.

Then something happened...

Before the surgeon walked out of the room, he brought up the X-ray on the screen and said "ok young man, we're getting tooth 1, 16, 17, and 32." While showing me this he was pointing to the screen and I noticed that tooth 1 and 32 was on one side while tooth 16 and 17 was on the other. I'm very big on signs and symbols because I know that God has no limits when it comes to His love and understanding. He speaks in so many ways. So after noticing that my "wisdom" teeth were labeled as 1, 32, 16, and 17, I knew something was there but I hadn't realized it yet. And then it clicked. As nervous as I was before this surgery, my spiritual light bulb lit up and I smirked. I smiled because it was in that private and personal moment right before I fell asleep that God assured me that He was with me. Right then and there I was assured of His covering. Being a follower of Christ, I know by faith that He died at the age of 33.

So where's the connection?

"Wisdom" tooth 1 and 32 was on the same side. Add them up, your sum is 33. "Wisdom" tooth 16 and 17 were on the other side. Add them up, the sum is also 33. No matter what your situation is or whatever situation you're in, when you have faith...the SUM of your equation will always be the SON. The pain was so excruciating but I know it had purpose connected to it. I found new levels of grace that day. Glory to God. Funny how the extraction of "wisdom" teeth lead to God teaching me more about wisdom. If something is withdrawn from your life, know that God is surely on His way with another deposit. Pain teaches you more about proverbs and weeping teaches you more about wisdom. I couldn't even speak physically that night but in my silence, God was loud and clear. No matter what you go through in life, take the strength from it. The weight of your trial determines the strength of your smile. The God Smile is the *Sonlight* that the seeds in your soul need to grow. It is the thing that gives power to your potential, it pushes you to your prime.

Mr. Prime says to Potential, the song you were humming, that's one of my favorite songs ever. The guy that made that song inspired me to bring you here. His name is Wale. I haven't met him but I've always been a huge fan. He's a super easy guy to relate to, especially since he's from the same area as you. He has endless entendre filled lyrics, a one of one fashion style, an immense sneaker collection that he refers to in plenty of his raps, but more importantly he raps from the soul... especially in that song you were humming. I love that song for many reasons but the title of it really does it for me. It makes me think if you could see God smile, what would it look like, more so what would it feel like?

Let me tell you about how it all started with this song. It was April 4, 2015, it was a Saturday, one that was extremely beautiful. There wasn't a cloud in the sky, the sky was as blue as the Caribbean seas and the weather was perfect. About 65 degrees with a high of 70. On this day Wale came to DC. He had a free concert for his fans on H Street NE. The concert took place in the AutoZone parking Lot. When I woke up on that morning I decided to attend the concert with some of my friends from college. When I first arrived on H Street, I was by myself. I was pretty familiar with the area because two of my close friends lived not too far away, in the River Terrace neighborhood. I also used to work for Metro Access as a paratransit driver, so I had grown a bit familiar with that area.

When I first pulled onto H Street, I could already hear the music and see how crowded the event was. H Street filled with restaurants, bars and other businesses, it was very difficult to find parking. While searching for parking my friend Jon, who was there already called and told me to go to the Sherwood Recreation Center and Elementary School and it would more than likely be some parking up there. Taking his advice, I found parking on the street in between the 9th and 10th Street block. I parked right in front of some houses that were on my right and the school was on my left. By now, it was about 3:15pm, I got out of my car and walked down to the concert. As I was walking, I thought about my senior year of college when Jon and I would sit and read through all of Wale's lyrics from his Folarin mixtape.

Approaching the AutoZone, Jon called me again, and told me to hurry up because it was getting crowded, quickly. Luckily, I was able to get into the concert and meet up with him. My other two friends Tysean and Hanani were also there but closer to the front than we were. Filled with excitement, restlessness, and enthusiasm, I was just embracing the moment and telling Jon that I was glad I could make it.

I kept looking in the sky on this day, admiring its beauty and just engulfed with the peaceful pleasantness it possessed. Once Wale came out, his song Legendary was playing and I was just happy to finally see him perform live. This concert was right after his fourth project released TAAN (The Album About Nothing). There is a song on the album titled *The God Smile;* my favorite song on the album, however, after this day the entire meaning and significance went to another level.

Midway through the concert I texted my friend Marcus and told him that the concert had not ended yet and I was telling him to hurry up so he could make it. At this point they were just letting people in, you no longer needed your RSVP. Marcus is one of my friends who I mentioned lived in the River Terrace neighborhood. He had to help someone move that morning and he wasn't sure he would make it to the concert. He hit me back shortly after, telling me he was on his way.

Once he arrived, Jon and I met up with him and we enjoyed the rest of the show together. I believe Wale was performing *The White Shoes* when he showed up. The end of the concert was approaching, and before it concluded, Wale looked up at the sky and said, *"The sun is out, go and shine your light on me, if you want to be blessed, put your hands in the sky."*

Right then I knew he was about to perform The God Smile and I now knew at that very moment why the day was that beautiful. When Wale said "the sun" I interpreted this to mean "the Son." Not only was "the sun" out, but "the Son" of God, Christ and His presence was present and He was shining His light. Not to mention, this was the Saturday before Easter, which is the day we celebrate His resurrection. "I'm thankful."

This song defined the day because I really felt like God was smiling and His light was shining. I was just thankful to be out there. At this point, the day was bliss, it was perfect. It looked like *heaven's afternoon.*

Once the concert ended, you could hear "88" one of Wale's songs off the album 'The Gifted' playing in the speakers. At this point Marcus, Tysean, Hanani, Jon, and I had all met up, still on the AutoZone parking lot. We all wanted to take a picture together before we left. Once we got our picture, we talked about linking up to watch the Michigan State vs. Duke and Kentucky vs. Wisconsin games that night. We had all planned to get together over Tysean's house to watch the games, but this plan, was however, unfortunately altered and interrupted.

None of us were parked near each other. So we dispersed. I was going to give Marcus a ride home so he and I started heading to my car. As we were walking, a police car slowly drove beside us on our left. He was driving at the speed we were walking. I noticed it and it looked fishy, but I had no reason to acknowledge it honestly, because neither one of us were doing anything wrong. Marcus noticed the officer and asked, "Bro wassup with him?"

I responded, "Yeah I don't even know, but we good." The officer made eye contact but proceeded to turn left while we made a right. Marcus saw my car and said, "There it is bro, I see it."

As we walked to the car we assumed everything was cool and got in the car. I turned and looked over my shoulder before crossing the street to get in the car and could still see the officer. Once we got in the car, before I even had the chance to start the car, Marcus said, "Bro, here he comes."

I looked up and saw the officer drive past the car and followed his car in my rearview and saw him make a sharp U-turn until I lost sight of it. When I lost sight of the car, Marcus could see it in his side mirror and he replied, "He's just sitting there at the corner." I didn't attempt to pull off because something wasn't right. After about fifteen to thirty seconds, the officer reappeared in my left side mirror and pulled his car in front of me at an angle, blocking me in. At this point, I was confused. I couldn't really believe this was happening, and it clearly had to be a mistake.

I looked in my mirror again and saw another police car pulling behind me also at an angle. I cracked my door slightly to look behind me. In a split second I heard an officer yell, "Don't step out of the f****** car, stay in the car! Put your hands on the steering wheel and look forward."

I responded, "Ok, yes sir."

As the officer yelled and approached the car, he had his gun drawn, in hand. Still in shock and confused, I completely lost attention to anything else and now, I'm only focused on what this officer is telling me. He yells "Step out of the car, slowly!"

I responded, "Yes sir, I'm going to slide out slowly because my phone is on my lap and I don't want it to hit the ground."

He yelled, "Get out of the car!"

I proceeded to follow his instructions and when I got out of the car he said "put your hands behind your head and lock your fingers." After I did this, he pushed me onto the hood of my car and began to frisk me. Aggressively searching me as if he knew I had something on me. His next words were, "where are you coming from?" I said "from the Wale concert, on H Street that just ended." (The concert ended at 5:00 so this was around 5:15-5:30). His response was "what's in the car? Do you have anything on you?" I immediately responded, "No sir, there is nothing in the car and I don't have anything on me. Continuing to be searched, I can see now that two more police vehicles have arrived and there are now four total police cars. I was then asked were there any narcotics in the car, I responded by saying "no sir there isn't and this must be some sort of mistake."

Marcus also had two officers on the passenger side of the car holding him and he was being frisked and thoroughly searched as well. The officer then asked me to go to the back and place my hands on my trunk and to spread my legs. I had my legs spread so wide that I could not feel whether my wallet was in my back pocket. The officer is now asking me where is my wallet and since I can't feel it because of how gripped my jeans were at this point from spreading my legs, I honestly didn't know. I told him that it was either in my back pocket or on the seat in the car.

Officers are now searching the car, going through every compartment really believing that we had whatever it was that they were looking for. While I had my hands on the trunk, I felt it pop open so I knew now they wanted to search the trunk, I slightly moved my left hand and as soon as I did that, the officer slammed my arm/hand right back on the trunk. I told him "sir it just popped open, he's trying to check it." He then asked me to step back and the trunk popped open. Another officer who was present came over but this one did not have on an actual police uniform, he was dressed in casual wear, with his badge around his neck like a detective of some sort. He came over to me and was talking to me while he began to search through the trunk. The first question he asked me was "whose car is this?" I responded by saying this is my deceased grandfather's car, but it is in my grandmother's name. I drive it every day so it pretty much belongs to me.

There was a duffle/traveling bag that I had in there from the night before that I had some extra clothes in because the night before I was in my cousin's wedding. The officer asked me what was in the bag and I told him nothing; just some belongings of mine, bath products, etc. He proceeded to go in the bag, went in a bag that was inside of that bag, opened up my dress shoes box and searched the inside of the shoes, etc. I mean every possible crack and crevice that there was that could be searched, he went through it. I was told to sit on the curb and then immediately told to stand back up. This same officer told me that he was now going to search me. I had my back to him first and then I faced him and as he searched my crotch area, he was grabbing so hard and feeling so hard for drugs that he actually was hurting my genitals, but I still remained calm and just didn't say anything until I was FINALLY asked "Do you know what is going on? Do you know what this is about?" I responded and said, "No sir I have no idea, I'm clueless."

He responded by saying, "Someone made a call and said that you guys were hustling on the street, and selling drugs out of this car." "I remained calm and said "sir, that has to be a mistake, a mix up, and you have the wrong guys, I don't touch drugs." Looking me square in my face this man asked me "Are you on parole? Do you have any warrants? Are you on probation?" I said "sir, I've never been arrested, never been to jail, nor had any encounters with the law." He then said ok you can sit back on the curb. While sitting on the curb I kept my hands extended outward because I didn't want anything to be mistaken. The officer behind me said "relax man, go ahead and relax." After about 5-10 minutes another cop came over and in a joking tone said, "Ok, well if y'all not on America's most wanted, you can go ahead and leave." I didn't think the joke was funny but I looked up behind me to confirm with the officer if I could stand or not and he said yes you can stand and go. The detective came over one last time and said "Thank you for your 100% cooperation, we'll be carrying on now." And that was it...

Although I may have had the right to ask questions, I did not feel any desire to do so in those moments. The crazy part about all of this is my heart never raced. It was like a peace surrounding me that never allowed me to fear because this was only a necessary trouble and test that was meant to enhance and strengthen my testimony. This incident was a couple weeks before Freddie Gray's death in Baltimore, MD, six officers were in the truck with him and six officers were present on this day.

However, Marcus and I both remained composed through this and I knew that we were both praying...our hearts were connected during this situation which I truly believe manifested a form of peace that governed the whole area. In other words, I analyzed this situation from more of a spiritual perspective than anything else. It was nothing the enemy could do to stop the resurrection, uprising and prospering of God. God has a grand way of defending you for His name's sake.

Last but not least, once we got back in the car and I started the car no words were exchanged between Marcus and me. He turned to #8 on Wale's album, 'The God Smile'.

"Through it all I illuminate, by Faith...Lord shine your light on me..."

"The devil's around the corner, it's all good because the God is living in you."

Something I've learned about the enemy is he always fights greatness in the beginning stages. The attack on you is that diligent because your destiny is that anointed. The truth of the matter is the burden is not going to break you, it is going to break you through. The last thing the adversary wants to see is the evolution of greatness happening in you. He does not want you to reach your *prime quality*. The call on your life bothers him deeply because the top floor of your greatness is Glory and God's glory is the enemies' grief. This is why the enemy wants to keep you locked in the basement. He does everything possible to keep your life in a stage of plight because he knows if you ever take flight, he would then lose sight of you and you would lose sight of him.

No matter what he tries to do to you, it all works out for your good when you love the Lord because all things are possible for those that believe. No matter how close the enemy is or what he plots, God is always closer and His plans always prevail. Keep this in mind, any problem that comes your way...God had to give it permission. We could have easily been another victim of police brutality, and in fact we were victims of racial profiling. Our names could have been hashtags on twitter. We could have been arrested. We could have been taken to jail. The cops could have stashed something in the car, they could have lied, they could have wanted to go further, they could have beat on us, it could have been a different way, a different day, and a different outcome...but God smiled.

This example along with countless others, serve as catalysts; having all contributed to my understanding of how all challenges, adversities, and troubles have a purpose. God's word is the last word, no matter what, which is why it's critical to do and say your piece then trust Him to give you peace. As painful as grief and frustration can be, my faith assures me that Glory is sure to follow because the bigger the mess the bigger the message.

Many years ago, day to day life was redefined for me once I encountered the true power and love of God. I always believed in God, always prayed, and always attended church services, but the understanding of life lessons and experiences is what really helped me graduate from a believer to a faith walker. My life became deeper, tests became harder, and trials became more intense. However, the most important thing is that my relationship with Christ became more personal, passionate, powerful, and prayer-filled. Life was not just about living any more, but about understanding, praying, seeing, seeking, talking, listening, helping, and doing everything that God would have me to do in a sincere and holy way.

As I continue to mature on many levels, my faith is steadily evolving and growing me into something I never knew I would be. There is always a new level to reach and a new mission to accomplish. Every bumpy road and high obstacle serves as a training course that has been set up for my prospering, even if it is disguised as pain.

The steps that God ordered for me helped me see things from a totally different perspective than my friends, family members, and even in some cases, enemies. Most importantly, through all of this, I not only experienced long days and tough tedious nights, but I have become a much stronger individual mentally, physically and spiritually. Simply put, my growth process has constructed my character and my character is developed constantly. Every day I am granted another day of life, something else is being added. The beauty in this is realizing that this is merely the beginning. This was hard to understand when up against certain circumstances, but now I can actually say I am proud of the pain and if it were not for the love and grace of God, I would not be here to even testify about His greatness, let alone give him Glory. The more intense your pursuit of God becomes, the more intricate your battlefield will be.

Stay the course.

THE PURPOSE OF QUESTIONS

"To Thine own Self Be True"

Potential sees problems a bit differently at this point. He feels thankful, he is grateful, he feels blessed. He extends gratitude to Mr. Prime and tells him how appreciative he is. Potential says, I thank you for talking with me and the patience you've had with me. I thank you for answering all of my questions. I don't have many left, but I do have a couple more. I ask questions because I'm intrigued and fed by your faith.

How are you able to answer all of my questions? I haven't heard you say "I don't know" to any of my questions, every answer has been something I can understand and apply to my life. How?

Mr. Prime answers by first saying, "It's an honor to be an ear for the heart that speaks. It's always an exchange because we pour into each other. However, consider the words of a rock. "But in your hearts revere Christ as Lord. Always be prepared to give an answer to everyone who ask you to give the reason for the hope that you have. But do this with gentleness and respect,"

Potential responds and says, a rock said that?

Mr. Prime smiles...

It's not that I know all of the answers, it's just me knowing that faith can fill in every blank and every response is spirit lead.

Whenever you feel like you don't know the answer or can't find the answer, trust in what you know to be true. Trust what has made you and gone into your life. The best thing might not always be the right thing but the right thing will always be the best thing. No situation can erase salvation so if you find it difficult to pray, rest in knowing that God's grace and mercy can smother the loudest scream even if it's silent. Remind yourself that He is all knowing, unlimited in power and everywhere all the time. So even if you can't pray, remember that He is the creator of your core and He knows the intentions of your soul, even when you can't move. His love outweighs anything in this life. What no man can tell you, He will place and affirm in your heart. All things can't be found, sometimes you have to let it find you. Lastly, never be afraid to be your strongest self because when things are at their worst, that's when the best can be found in you. Pros and cons are just symbols of balance, whether you're right or you're wrong...you're His.

I understand that practicality is a part of life so in some instances faith may not be that strong or even exist in some capacities. So if significantly less faith is a part of the equation, find out what it is that you love more than anything in this world. Ask yourself or someone else what is it that they feel is worth living for and dying for. Figure that out because no matter what situation you're in, when you have passion you have purpose and no problem can change that. No situation can blind a man's heart, so even when you can't see you still have vision. No matter what decisions are made, moving forward is the only way you can reach new terrains, new territory, new trials, and new triumphs. Doing nothing is not an option but moving forward is to attain peace.

Often-times we are faced with questions. We always have to make decisions, some weighing more than others but nonetheless, we have to decide on certain things day in and day out. Whether it be what we eat, what we wear, or where we go. People make decisions daily, while sometimes depending on others to help us find the answers. However, when dealing with internal battles, mental whirlwinds, and matters of the heart…sometimes another person's answers just don't quite give us the satisfaction or fulfillment we are seeking. A person can only provide an answer the best way they understand the situation. No one can answer it how you would answer it unless they know everything about it like you do. You never know what a person is going through. The worst thing you can do is belittle their problems and discredit their feelings. You'll never truly understand a person's perspective because you didn't walk in their shoes. At least give them an ear and let them tell you where they've been or where they are. If you do that you'll find out where they are trying to go.

For example, you can be at church and hear a really great sermon that uplifts your spirits, but the very next day that spiritual high can be gone, and you're still facing the same obstacles and unanswered questions. A person can give you advice that may very well be honest, true, and helpful but it may not console you completely. On the flip side you may get some advice from someone that is terrible. It may not align with your principles, thoughts, or even how you feel. People may have similar outlooks and opinions as you but no one will ever have the exact same experience as you. Your experience is pretty much what determines your perspective and your perspective greatly influences your reality.

What is it that will bring you what you want? What are you chasing after? What is it that you really need? What will change your life for the better? What will change the lives around you for the better? What will get you to the next level? What will keep you focused? What will push you to persevere? What will make you feel confident? What will inspire you? What will motivate you? What will keep you humble?

What will change your mind? What should you do? What will bring you happiness? What is your why? What is your driving force? What is your place of peace? What do you want forever? What do you want your legacy to be? What matters to you? What are your morals? What do you value? What do you long for? What do others not know about you that make you who you are? What are your strengths? What are your weaknesses? What do you remember? What will you always remember? What do you wish you could change? What hurts you? What helps you? What do you want to know? What do you regret, or do you have any regrets? What scares you? What do you want to be? What do you love more than anything in this world? What do you feel is worth living for and dying for? How far are you willing to go?

Life is full of questions. If you want to find the answers, discover the truth in you. The purpose of a question is to meet the truth. Questions stimulate a person's thinking, leading them to answer questions with realness and honesty that will ultimately lead to an understanding. The best questions we can ask are the questions we ask ourselves. Looking at ourselves in the mirror is something that is so powerful but misperceived. When we look in the mirror we see our reflection, but the image the mirror gives us is one of our physical selves. The mirror shows us our appearance and how we look on the outside. However, the mirror does not show what's on the inside.

Questions when asked of ourselves and answered with truth develop similar power as a mirror. A mirror gives us our reflection but questions cause us to reflect. When we as people reflect, we enter a stage of self-examination, a stage where hopefully the truth will sharpen the clarity of our answers. The power of a question lies in the truth of its answer. The more truth you provide for yourself, the deeper your reflection will be and the better you will understand what is inside of you. The more we lie to ourselves, the blurrier we make our vision. Our reflection then becomes deception. There's no worse person you could deceive than yourself. When we lie to ourselves we lead ourselves further away from peace and deeper into pain. We constantly hurt ourselves when we aren't real with ourselves. When we aren't real with ourselves, we may be unknowingly, a fraud, to everyone else. Give yourself what you feel you deserve. Make peace your daily pursuit. You owe you, your best.

I remember earlier you asked, what if your best isn't good enough and how do you maintain? Is it possible? You also asked, what do you do if pain beats you down and tries to paralyze you?

Try to focus on not just doing your best for you, but doing your best for God. Your best is always good enough for Him, because He knows what He put inside of you. You only do a disservice to Him when you doubt yourself because when you doubt yourself, you're basically doubting Him. The scriptures tell us that "without faith, it is impossible to please Him."

Never stop driving. There is direction in disappointment. Disappointment directs you closer to your destiny.

And to your question, yes, it is possible to maintain. It starts with a willingness in the mind that is reflected in your heart. Once the heart accepts that pursuit, your soul agrees and your love is then the proof. I know I can't rise to my destiny unless I am able to survive this place and everything it comes with because even with everything going on here, I know it is all a part of His plan. Whether it be failure or success, it's all necessary because all things work together for the good of those that love God and are called according to His purpose. I rest in my uncertainties because my faith makes it possible to believe, when everything and everyone else around tells me it's impossible. I'm here on purpose. Right now at this time for a reason. I'm learning to even rest in pain because that's the thing that makes joy feel so good.

Real love for God never allows one's hope to be eliminated. It may defer but it is never destroyed when you truly love Him. "Hope deferred maketh the heart sick, but a longing fulfilled is a tree of life." My hope is in Christ and even with the uncertainties and fluctuations of life's circumstances, my constant stability is found in Him. That doesn't mean I don't notice the world and what goes on, but instead of it making me doubt, it solidifies my convictions by confirming my call. The current state of the world serves as confirmation for your gifts. You are God's smile. The world needs you here to make a difference in a way that only you can. If joy is tailor made then pain is too and I'm down to wear the suit in both seasons. My desires are strengthened by adversity and the intensity of the trials have given me a touch of madness that makes me more intentional with everything. All in all, I maintain it by telling myself to never stop believing because my soul trust my spirit and my spirit trust my heart and my heart trust my mind because my mind is always on Him.

You can't walk by faith and live in fear.

My darkest days made me who I am. In every part of me, it was the storms that washed away what wasn't me and brought to life what was in me. Even in knowing that more dark days are ahead…to a believer darkness can become a playground, where you find that the light is in you. Lights are most useful in darkness.

For we walk by faith, not by sight. The strength of your storm determines how big your rainbow will be. Find the beauty in your storm. When you're built differently, your path will be different. When you are built differently, your pain will be different. When you are built differently, you win different. A storm will show you how special you are because you didn't know you would survive it. You find out more of your unknown capabilities when you have to exercise your known abilities. More about you becomes known when you are thrown in the unknown.

Faith is the fuel for the drive. Never stop. Your purpose is depending on you. Your prime is depending on you. Establish real expectations for yourself. Know what you expect of you. As your drive deepens, your journey will carry you to newer destinations and you will see more as you keep going. There are so many things we hear that hold incredible depth but so many fear the dive. The stronger you get in the mind, the more you can handle in the heart. Your heart is your engine. Every beat is another mile. How far you willing to go?

Your testimony will tell where you've been. Sometimes God wants you in the driver's seat and at other times He wants you in the passenger seat. He teaches you how to drive and how to ride. When He has you in the driver's seat He's working on your concentration and increasing your focus. He builds your patience when there's traffic. He teaches you how to pay attention and to understand how important defense is in life. In some cases an accident may not even be your fault. He teaches you how to stay in your own lane and not drift. The driver's seat teaches you about responsibility. You have to listen to directions to get to your destinations. When He has you in the driver's seat, He is teaching you the importance of rest. How so? Because to get to your destined place you can't fall asleep. God shows so much.

Potential says, so what about the passenger seat?

Mr. Prime responds by saying, if you know how to ride, you understand what it means to be driven. Some roads God just wants you to observe and absorb. Why? Because sometimes He wants you to really just see what He is bringing you through. God elevates you by carrying you to higher places. As you ride you will see how every mile is a deeper message of purpose from Him. He puts you in the passenger seat sometimes to teach you how to drive better. He shows you different routes and roads less traveled. When you ride with Him, you never have to stop to get gas because the thing that keeps the car going is what I've been talking to you about this entire time; your faith. Your drive doesn't alter your destination, it just makes your journey greater.

Keep raising your own bar. Every day the drive is unexpected and each day becomes more and more indescribable. I've asked out loud, Lord where are you taking me? Constantly going for more, doing more, seeing more, giving more, enduring more, thanking more, being more. It's amazing to see what can happen when one believes. Don't worry about anyone measuring your obedience, your patterns, your commitments, your drive or your time. Don't grow weary in well doing. Your fruit will be the proof. It doesn't matter what they think. Don't let anything that anyone else is thinking make you lose focus.

Your dream requires a rare vision and a rare vision is going to see things differently. It's no way that it can't. Don't compromise nothing about your call. Focus man. Don't pay attention to how long it's taking, keep pushing. Don't worry about nothing, know that God got it all. Just do your part. Believe in yourself man. Believe in yourself. Believe in yourself. Faith in God should produce confidence in you. Believe in yourself!

As soon as you doubt, start over. Doubt is a distraction, but faith keeps you focused. Believe man! You're so close to a new level. It's right there. Do not stop. Do not turn around. You have come so far. Drive man, go through with it. God gives you a revelation so you can be the manifestation of the thing He revealed to you. IT IS YOU! Live like your life depends on it. Keep rising above anything that isn't aligned with your purpose or your peace. You are going higher.

All your life you are working towards completing the picture. Sometimes your pieces fit, sometimes they don't. But every piece has purpose, even if you haven't found it yet. And the greatest clue about the final picture is you see it every day...because it's you.

BORN TO LOVE

Learning the principles of love teaches you the purpose of life. Leaving the cage that had my mind bound and kept self-love away, is when I realized the power and importance of intentionally loving who you are. Loving yourself is letting God direct you toward your destiny. I had to learn to love myself on purpose. I had to learn to love myself enough to allow God to show me what it is that He put in me and at the same time be willing to understand it. I had to pray and ask God to show me how to love myself better and not feel bad about it.

Potential, the very first question you ever asked me was, "How do I reach my greatest self?" Mr. Prime responds and says, by realizing that you become more of it daily. You reach your greatest self by realizing that you never stop becoming it. You might not get it all right the first time but you get better each time, constantly learning through each stage. Perfection in Christ is daily progression within yourself. When you trust God's grace over the laws you hear, you see that forgiving yourself is the best thing you can do. When you go your hardest, you learn how to work your smartest. If you want to love someone wonderfully, you have to love yourself perfectly and talk to God honestly. Let the love you have for yourself and God be displayed in how you love others, and allow the love you have for others show how you desire to be loved. You are valuable and you must see the value in yourself. Liberate your love.

Fast-forwarding through much of their conversation they are now at a point of heightened awareness. They are thinking differently. They've been introduced to something called a Christ Consciousness, and the conversation continues.

Potential says, how do you make it when it's so dark? How can you see when it's so dark? How can you live when the world told you, you were too dark?

Mr. Prime responds, it's never too dark because that's what you were birthed from. There is a light in you and if it weren't for darkness, you would have never been created. So I'll say again, the light is in you. It's a different type of light though. It's the light of life, it shows you the way, and it always tells you the truth. And in regard to the world, if you believe in Him, then you are the light of the world because if you believe in Him then you are in Him and He is in you. And long ago He said, "While I am in the world, I am the light of the world." So in essence, you are an instrument of light that He uses to shine for Him in the world.

Potential asks, how do you know that?

Mr. Prime follows up saying: Because in the beginning God created the heavens and the earth and the earth was formless and empty, darkness was over the surface of the deep and the spirit of God was hovering over the waters. And God said, "Let there be light," and there was light. God saw that the light was good, and he separated the light from the darkness.

Potential responds, but how do you know?

Mr. Prime says...because anything is possible for one who believes and I believe it. I believe that I know because I know that I believe. Faith is my fortress.

Potential takes his last and final pause and as he parts his lips as their conversation is coming to a close...he says, Mr. Prime my life has changed, I feel like I've just grown up. My life seems to have come alive, I feel like I finally get what you've been speaking to me about for so long. I think I understand what it means to reach my prime and to know my prime quality. This is my last question sir, and the only one that hasn't been answered...

What if I die?

These were the questions of a heart, one that had a beat so distinct that it had a supernatural instinct to effortlessly save souls.

After you look at all you've done, all you've overcome, all you've learned, and all you've received. My only answer left for you, is to love. Give it all back. Sow to grow and give to live. Teach people the sound of your beat because that sound is incomparable. It encompasses absolutely everything that we've been through. It continues to beat through pain while at the same time knowing how to jump for joy. It has cried blood but it has a God smile. It has survived darkness by simply becoming the light. It has a rhythm that knows how to dance in the rain. It's nothing it can't do. The blind can see it, the deaf can hear it, and the heartless can feel it. Tell them all about it, let it be seen in how you move, how you live, how you speak, how you endure and push through. Let it be seen in how you manage, how you maneuver, and how you master things. Teach the lessons you've learned about respect and character, about hard work and how it's good for the soul. Be a grand example of integrity, and strength like nothing ever seen before. Tell your testimony and how it wasn't formed until you had a test. Tell them about how you made it through. But when you tell them, make sure the language is love because that language is the language that all hearts can hear. It's the language that needs no translator. Even the illiterate can understand it. Your heart has the potential to do anything because everything flows from it.

And whenever you get down and discouraged, just remember, I was beaten too, I was spit on too, I was betrayed too, enslaved too, stripped too. They arrested me too, locked me up too, they lied on me too, hung me on a tree too, they tried to kill me too. But my friend, it is when you die…that you really live. You die to rise because you were born to love.

Your Love is the language of this land, let it live and you'll never lose because everything you do flows from your heart.

Smile, because the Joy you contain inside is what everything and everyone around you needs and what they want. Reflect on everything you've been through. Your smile is the enemies trial, and the bigger the trial, the stronger the smile.

Be a beacon of Peace, because you have that same power to create harmony amongst hearts.

Show people how to endure, and go the distance. With every mile your heart has traveled, you've left facts everywhere. Your love has the fuel of fortitude and Forbearance.

Never underestimate your Kindness because when you are kind you have power and when you are kind you know how to serve. Kindness is a key that was molded by the Master.

Believe that you are already good because when God created the light, He saw that it was good and your Goodness is what makes you great.

Understand that your Faithfulness to Him is why He raises you over so much. He loved you first and has been faithful ever since.

Keep your touch so Gentle that everything you touch only grows into glory.

Be so Composed that nothing moves you because you know who you are and you know who is in control.

Against these things, there is no law because no one can ever lock up your love. To think with Christ is to be so woke that you live in a constant dream. A dream where you're alive and He constantly speaks to you never allowing you to sleep on yourself. Your love is real liberation, and you are the manifestation of it.

Last but not least, never forget to love yourself. Be free.

From all of this, Mr. Prime says his final words to Potential...

In some of my grandfather's last days he laid on his hospital bed and told me, "P's & Q's brother."

Potential grieved and grieved realizing that their conversation was coming to a close. He wept until his tears created a puddle. The puddle formed quickly because he wept so hard, but the puddle had a present for Potential. He gave Potential his reflection. When Potential looked down and saw his reflection, he saw Mr. Prime. He then realized that he had been talking to himself the entire time. He smiled and then he looked up and when he looked up, he saw his grandfather.

"In the midst of Your love, carried by the currents of purpose...surfing on the waves of wisdom, sailing to the shores of understanding. God, thank You for teaching me how to express what lies deep. The depth of Your understanding is unsearchable but I know the depth of one's destiny is discoverable. Pursue your peace... "

EPILOGUE

The *Case of Craig: One African-American Male's Values and Upbringing*

I interviewed my friend Craig in an effort to complete a class project. We talked for about 50 minutes one Tuesday morning. Craig is a Christian African-American male, in his mid-20s. Craig is already my friend, we are both Christian males in our mid-20s, and I interact with many African-Americans, including the majority of my students. However, I still believed that I could gain perspective from interviewing Craig because when I was a child, teenager, and college student I had limited associations with African-Americans; further, today there are only a couple African-Americans with whom I spend time outside of work and class. I am aware that I have a lot left to learn, especially about family dynamics and value systems, so although I was optimistic about my interview with Craig, I had no idea of what to expect from his answers.

The interview began with me asking the first suggested question, "Can you please tell me what you find most valuable in your life?" Craig answered, "The most valuable thing in my life is my relationship with God, completely, because it's worth everything... The value in that is what brings worth and value to everything else" (personal interview, March 21, 2017). When asked to describe this relationship in detail, he listed many things encompassed by this relationship, including how he lives his daily life, sharing and receiving love, having joy in good and bad times, having inner peace and the fruits of the spirit, including goodness, kindness, gentleness, composure, and forbearance, and finally having a foundation for whatever life brings.

I validated Craig's answer but pressed him to identify another value beyond this all-encompassing one. He thought for a while and decided that, outside of God, he most cared about "character," meaning one's identity, inside and out, at its true, vulnerable core. He distinguished this from one's reputation, which can be formed from things that are not true. Craig explained that the value he assigns to character includes having a true character that is "receptive, approachable, respectful, honest, willing to grow, and patient." This character would or should be present when at one's best, when learning, when teaching, and generally all the time.

Once again, I thanked Craig for his response and acknowledged it. However, once again I explained my growing curiosity: he had chosen two great values (relationship with God, and character) that each encompass many qualities, but if he had to pick only one quality or characteristic for himself that he most values working towards, what would it be? To this, his answer (after thinking quietly for a while) was, "I try to love better every day, whether loving God, myself, or others," and so the answer would be "to be loving, that's my biggest value." Craig predicted my next question and said, "Okay, but what does that look like... hmm... it is my daily conversations." I asked him what about his daily conversations he you working on to make them more and more loving. This involved some discussion, but ultimately resulted in the answers of transparency and vulnerability; Craig seemed to experience a sudden insight that at the heart of it, what he most values and is working towards is being "bold enough to reveal my authentic self, who I really am, even if it ain't pretty." A couple more minutes of conversation revealed that what Craig most prizes as a value is a sense of integrity and alignment between his relationship with God, his core character, and his daily life and conversations.

Then, I shifted the conversation to his upbringing by asking him where he got these values. His initial reaction was to give God the credit: "I got these values not only from the people that God put in my life, but the places he's carried me, the experiences I've had, the short-comings I've had, the triumphs I've had; I got them from every season, from the best and from the worst, from the blessings and the burdens, from my upbringing."

I asked him to zero in on his upbringing and tell me a little more about that. What I learned about Craig's upbringing is that he lived with his mother, siblings, and two grandparents, while his father was incarcerated. In his home, he felt that love was the constant umbrella over everything, the backdrop for all the interactions he experienced. In this setting, he described receiving "so much encouragement, support, selflessness, nourishment," with these values being modeled by his mother and grandparents. He remembered feeling the love clearly because he "was simply taken care of – having a nice dinner, gifts at Christmas, and conversations were they were really present and involved… and they would be on me to do my best." In terms of encouragement, he remembered his mother saying "I love you" frequently and asking him, "How are you doing?" Similarly, he remembered his grandfather communicating love by always telling him "P's and Q's" when he left home each morning, meaning, "never forget the manners and behavior we have taught you." Although he remembered being disciplined, such as being grounded or spanked, Craig recalled all of these things (not only being told he was loved and taken care of, but also the discipline, reminders to be on his manners, and pressure to do his best) as part of a clear atmosphere in which he was certain that he was loved, that he was accepted, and that discipline and reminders came to direct and guide him towards higher standards that his family believed him capable of. In particular, discipline came in a warm, not cold way, with an explanation of why the particular thing (such as listening) is important.

I mentioned to Craig that research has suggested that firm discipline in families of color is sometimes oriented towards optimizing that the child's behavior for his/her survival in a racist society, and I asked him about whether or not he saw his family's use of discipline in this light, and whether he was aware of those racial considerations as a child. He said yes to both questions, and explained that discussion of race in his family growing up had two main focuses: giving him appreciation, and giving him awareness.

In terms of the racial awareness he learned from his family, Craig explained that the main message he received was, "There's gonna be some things you go through that aren't right, are unjust, totally, but always maintain your composure, know how to convey love... manage to move on... The world is a lot tougher fight than the house, but we want to train you here so that when you get out there you can stand on the things you were taught." He also remembered stories from his grandparents, who grew up when racism was more socially permissible. These stories came with a tone of "This is what I got/persevered through; I'm only telling you because I experienced it." His grandfather, who was in the Navy, told him a story about white lifeguards draining a pool after he and some fellow black officers used it; his grandmother told him about the comments her white supervisor at her government job. The expectation was that Craig, too, would face discrimination but be prepared to stay in touch with his true character throughout and keep moving forward.

I asked if he remembered the first time he became aware of his racial identity or that society involved discrimination. Craig responded that "there was no peak, my racial awareness grew gradually, with experiences of seeing bullying and other interactions." At this point, he chose to mention that as a child, part of his growing awareness included wrestling with his father being in prison. Although it was tough, this yielded him several insights. First, because his family needed to explain to him where his father was, his "upbringing included the fact that incarceration was a possibility if I didn't do what I was supposed to, and even more still, it can happen even if you're doing everything right." Second, although there was a natural temptation to resent his father's absence, this helped him appreciate the love-and-God-focused upbringing he received: he was able to choose not to resent his father, because "I was raised to understand that resentment is not what your spirit needs to develop to who God wants you to be." Instead, visits to his father showed Craig "the importance of all the umbrellas I was learning (character, love, relationship with God, joy, peace, etc.)."

Running out of time, I showed Craig a few potential questions and asked him to pick which he would most prefer to answer in the following minutes. He read them carefully, thought for a moment, and chose the question "Can you please tell me about a time in your life when you experienced discrimination and the impact this experience had on your life?"

He then began a very clear story with the disclaimer, "I think discrimination was a part, but not all, of this story I am going to tell you." Here is the story, as captured in my notes while it was related to me by Craig:

April 4, 2015, I was leaving an outdoor free Wale concert

downtown. I was there with my college buddies, and afterward I was taking one of them home; while we were walking to the car, a white police officer saw us; I didn't zone in on it because we weren't doing anything wrong, but he was driving at the same speed as we were walking. When we reached the corner, we went to the right, but he turned away to the left, so I thought nothing more of it. Then, when we got in our car, he was back with three or four other police cars blocking us in. He came up to us with a gun, used vulgar language, slammed me on the hood and aggressively searched my body, giving us no explanations at this point.

My buddy who was with me is usually passionate and emotional, but this day he was composed and silent; they separated us and had us on the curb, with all sorts of embarrassment. Then an official police detective came and was asking us, "what's going on, where you coming from?" This was right after, like a few days after what happened with Freddie Gray, so I was saying to myself, "even if you in the right, you gotta survive it before you address it," but in my mind I was thinking "You know God loves you, you know what your family taught you, your manners, stay composed."

Then the detective searched me again, went through all the car compartments (illegally), kept asking me what was going on, and I answered calmly that I didn't know, and where we had come from, and that we hadn't done anything wrong. If it weren't for my calm demeanor, things may have gone differently. Then, on his radio, he heard that the person he was looking for was on the next block; he thanked us for our 110% cooperation and told us we could go. One of the officers made a joke about how "we could go as long as we weren't on the 100 most wanted list," but yeah, it wasn't funny to us.

So ultimately, I think it was at least partly an experience of discrimination. Not all of the officers were white, the first one was, but there were some black ones there too by the end. However, I do think that if I was raised in a different house, and had more aggression, it could have gone very differently. My buddy shared with me later that the reason he was calm and composed was because he was with me, and he knows how important composure is to me. So it might have also gone different for him if I wasn't there.

At this point, we had run out of time, and I was just able to thank Craig for his candor and vulnerability, give him a chance to look over my notes for any potential misinterpretations, and thank him again for his time. My experience listening to Craig left me with a few different take-aways and surprises. I had known that his relationship with God is the most important part of his life, but hearing it come up so readily as a factor in his stories demonstrated to me how it functions to guide and orient his life. Specifically, I noticed how he mentioned God's plan for him as the reason he avoided resenting his father, and God's love for him as the very first thought he used to calm himself down when mistreated by the police. This demonstrated the depth to which his faith is integrated into his thoughts and actions, rather than simply something he does on Sundays or talks about to others.

In addition, it was good for me to hear about the ways that love was shown in Craig's household growing up. Sometimes, I hear stories from my African-American students about their parents disciplining them in a blunt or cold way, and I have seen this portrayed in the media and film industry as well. Learning about the tenderness in Craig's home helped counter this stereotype.

Finally, learning about his father being incarcerated, the racial stories and awareness shared with him as part of his upbringing, and his experience being wrongfully humiliated by police gave me a greater appreciation for Craig's resilience and commitment to his positivity and faith. Before this interview, I had consistently experienced Craig's faith as bright, energetic, and unfailingly optimistic; he has always seemed to have a sunny view of the world. I have had the privilege of talking with him as he dealt with several major setbacks and dreams deferred that hurt and upset him, but never made his commitment to positivity and faith seem to waver. It is sometimes hard for me to relate to such optimism. While I greatly respect Craig and his faith, and greatly appreciate his friendship and candor, the cynic in me had previously wondered whether his unflagging posture of gratitude and positivity perhaps indicated that he had not yet been forced to struggle with any truly dark or challenging life experiences that could potentially shatter a person's optimism. However, learning that Craig has indeed journeyed through his grandparents' and mother's stories of racism, a childhood of learning to show compassion and love to an incarcerated father, and personal experiences of violent racism shows me that the cynical voice in my mind is wrong. The grateful, positive posture Craig maintains is not an untested Pollyanna-ish attitude, but rather a real, enduring manifestation of the values he was raised to embrace: "There's gonna be some things you go through that aren't right, are unjust, totally, but always maintain your composure, know how to convey love."

—Peter A. Sanneman
Loyola University Maryland

ACKNOWLEDGMENTS

My heart overflows as I reflect on all of this. There's a profound level of gratitude that rest in my spirit. My intellect alone can't process my level of thankfulness, which is why in this moment I am truly and solely depending on my heart to do the talking.

There are so many people I've met in my life. So many people who have impacted my life. So many people who have meant so much to me. People I've had the pleasure of knowing and even people who have impacted my life who I've yet to meet personally. I don't know how I can thank everyone, but if I've ever been a part of you and you've ever been a part of me, if we ever shared anything, I thank you truly from my heart.

To the author and finisher of my faith. My Lord and Savior, Jesus Christ, thank You. I thank God for making His love brand new every single day. To God be all the Glory for all of the things He has done, is currently doing, and things to come.

To my family, I wouldn't trade my upbringing for the world; My Grams and only grandparent I have left; Christine Glover – Grandma's hands…I'll always hold on to "This too shall pass", my little brother Amir Jennings… (My young Alchemist aka Mir), and my stepfather Anthony Jennings… (Antman 31).

To my extended family; my cousins, aunts, uncles, god-parents and god-siblings.

To my sisters Taiyla, Arniece, and Konica; I love you all so much. To my younger brother Tyler; I love you champ.

To my dearest brothers, those who I had the pleasure of climbing a mountain with. Tysean Ellerbe, Jonathan Alvarez 99, Remington J. Culver, Marcus TA. Dixon, Hanani Felton aka Bo, Sean Davis aka LeftHandedSun, Casteel "Steely" Johnson, Taijai "King Nige" Alexander, Mr. "Chrisss" aka Tick, and Antwan Jermaine Smith. In the words of my grandfather, "You know what we got."

To my brother and my Ace, Armani Mason-Callaway aka Mase and the Callaway family.

   We laugh and joke about it all the time bro, but the truth is, you giving me Hill Harper's book after high school graduation forever blessed me. We were truly young brothers learning how to MANifest our destiny. Bro, thank you for selflessly helping me that final week in May 2009, what many never knew...we understood. I thank God for our memories and praise God for our futures. May Tre' continue to rest forever in eternity with the King. My big bro, who I'll one day meet. Till the end fam.

To Darius Arrington and Mr. & Mrs. Arrington. Family stretches wide and I'm happy to have always been a part of yours and you all a part of mine. With deep love and forever appreciation.

Chris Townsend—my brother, I'll never forget senior year in high school when you told me "Passion for the Lord, triumphs all logic." Nobody listened to BACK & TOB like us man lol. Love you forever.

To my bro Harley White, I will never forget that song...I love you fam.

My brother for life, Jerome Couplin (I know legends)

To the author of "A Spirit of Perseverance" & "365 Ways Through 365 Days," Earl Jackson, my bro. I don't know what else to say other than thank you for simply being who you are. Our connection was so organic and thrives off its genuineness. I'm forever grateful for how you believed in me and how you helped me really execute my dream. Thank you for our conversations and time spent. I thank God for you. Thank you bro and I love you.

To my Empowerment Temple family, the church where indescribable glory reigns.

Brothers I'll never forget whose handprints will always be on my heart. My childhood best friend Roger Parker, Nygee Quan Carmichael, and Princeton Tate.

To the women who believed in me and blessed me when they knew and didn't know.

To my best friend, my peace, and daily reason for my heart's smile, a very special Janay Boughton. I love you (Eternally Always) ▲♥.

To my cousin D'aira Thompson, never forget how strong you are. By blood you're my cousin, but by love you're my sister. I love you. The best is yet to come.

All my love and thanks: to my big sis who I love dearly, RoSharon Ingram, Jasmine A. Johnson my friend you already know #ALLGLORY, Mela Lawson—Literally my soul glowing sister in Christ who is the absolute realest. Thank you for your light, love, and prayers. Caitlin Harris—you were there the day I found the Alchemist and you believed in my dream. You and Jack boy haha I love you. Renata Malionek—My friend, we were Moreau Fellows together and years ago you believed in me and this dream and I just want to say thank you.

To my friend forever Mikea Nelson and her parents Mr. Nelson and Mrs. Nelson, for always treating me like a son. Thank you for your love.

To my 6th grade teacher, Mrs. Archer, you were my mom away from home and I love you forever. Thank you for going the extra mile for me.

To my very first supervisor at the Bureau of Engraving and Printing, Mr. Wallace Goosby. I love you forever. Memories of you still make me smile. You were like another grandfather to me. Our conversations were something I looked forward to everyday. Your example blessed my soul forever and I will never forget you.

To my neighbors, the Briggs Family.

To Mr. Stephan Sutton—You've taught me so much, but the thing that always stuck the most was "everyone wants to drive, but few enjoy the ride." Thank you for telling me it's a journey and not a destination. Thank you for everything.

To my entire Bishop McNamara High School family, every teacher, staff member, coach, classmate, student and alum. My home away from home. I love you deeply, for there is no place like McNamara. With sincere and special thanks To Dr. Marco Clark you have no idea of how your kindness and compassion has forever blessed and changed my life. Dr. Robert Van Der Waag, Dr. Nigel Traylor, Mr. George London, Mr. Roland Grimes, Dr. Victor Shin, Mr. Darryl Holloman, Mr. Peter Sanneman, Mrs. LaSandra Hayes, Mrs. Saiedeh Khalili, and Mrs. Lise Carver.

To my Alma Mater, Mount St. Mary's University. A place where I met lifelong friends who are my family and the place where I truly grew. With special thanks and love to Mr. Randall Phyall, my big brother.

To the entire Unity Barbershop. One of my favorite places on this earth. With special thanks to Coach Rick Taylor, Coach Tim Taylor, and my barber Mr. Don Williams.

To my inspirations:
• Paulo Coelho (author of The Alchemist)
• Hill Harper (Author of Letters to a Young Brother: MANifest your Destiny)
• My pastor and spiritual leader in Christ, Jamal H. Bryant
• LeBron James
• Tony Lewis, Jr.
• Wale

- Rakim
- My childhood favorite rapper Lil Wayne
- The ANF Action Figure up in Philly (Keep Driving & Never Give Up! Believe wholeheartedly! Keep chipping away! Train as if your life depends on it because it actually does!) You're the greatest soldier!

Thank you to the beautiful soul, my artist and designer of my book cover Raven Best, and thank you to my brother Marcus J. Williams who captured the images as this dream came to fruition.

To my Uncle Phillip and my Aunt Tammi. Words cannot express my appreciation for each of you. Unc you are more than an Uncle, you wear many hats and I am proud to be your nephew! You are the greatest and I love you so much! I have one more thing to say...THAT SAME POWER!

To my Uncle Albert- you have been another grandfather to me, I can't express how much your example has meant to me. There is nothing like talking sports with you. Another example I was blessed with to see how a man is supposed to be. I love you Unc.

To my editor/aunt/godmother/motivator/counselor Dr. Lesia M. Banks! This would NOT have happened without you! Thank you for your time, your love, your selflessness! You are my family! I would have never thought that my grandma Mildred Hines' transition to her heavenly home would have led to our reconnection. Our connection resurfaced for God had it set at that perfect time. I love you grandma Mildred.

To my Papa Paul Hines, may grandma and you dance forever in Heaven with the angels. I love you.

Thank you to everyone who I've ever met. Every conversation, every connection, every mentor, every mentee, everybody who ever contributed to me. My heart overflows. Thank you for those who believed in me and my book. Thank you for the encouragement, the uplift, the support, everything.

Dad—I thank you for believing in my dream and supporting me in any and every way you could. Never will I ever forget, "you're my latest and my greatest inspiration." Thank you for always being that to me and I love you.

To my Mother, Tuesday Glover Jennings, my core, my foundation to the first person I ever loved. The first person that ever showed love to me. There will never be enough words to describe my thoughts toward you. I'll never be satisfied with my sentiments which is why my heart will forever display and express my love for you for as long as I live. Your love is one of a kind and I'm just eternally grateful for you. Thank you for your constant outpouring of love, selflessness, support, honesty, help, smiles, encouragement, everything. Thank you for showing me how to love. Thank you for always being there. My appreciation for you is beyond my own understanding. I am truly me because of you. Thank you for being superwoman. You are and will always be my every day blessing. Forever and always.

To my Grandfather—Pop, there's one thing left to say... "You know what we got, P's & Q's brother."

From the bottom of my heart, to everyone, Thank You.

ABOUT THE AUTHOR

C raig Glover Hines is a man who truly has a heart for ministry and the youth. The Glory of God is really his daily motivation. Graduating from Mount St. Mary's University in 2013 with a BA in Communications and Minor in Theology, Craig seeks to make a lasting impact in the lives of students and people anywhere God leads him. Craig is also a graduate of Bishop McNamara High School, class of 2009, where he currently serves as a youth counselor, committed mentor, and Freshman Seminar teacher. As an avid sports fan, he is also one of the moderators of Fellowship of Christian Athletes (FCA) at Bishop McNamara.

In 2011, he was awarded the Washington District of Columbia College Success Foundation's "Team Leader/Peer Mentor of the year Award" recognizing awesome impact. While at Mount St. Mary's University Craig co-founded the Men's Empowerment Club, an organization with a mission to unite young men and enhance the overall camaraderie on campus through effective communication, faith discussions, community service initiatives, and, simply, the many realities of life. Craig believes that the trials and tribulations of life are truly what builds character, forms unity, and strengthens faith.

No matter the audience, Craig consistently expresses his desire to connect to a purpose greater than himself, which is drawn directly from Christ's mission for his life. During his senior year of undergraduate studies, Craig demonstrated unparalleled passion for guiding his peers toward their self-discovery and personal empowerment. While living a life based on character and identity development, Craig displays a genuine care and rapport with the peers he interacts with.

Craig's genuine personality, care for others, and unyielding faith in God has earned the respect of anyone and everyone he encounters. In a letter of recommendation to divinity school the writer described Craig as highly intelligent, disciplined, selfless, driven, and one of the most gifted students he had ever met. Craig's high level of integrity and standard of character instills a deep sense of trust among all whom he encounters. He consistently demonstrates the qualities of an outstanding servant, dedicated learner, and faith-driven leader.

Craig plans to not only write more books but also pursue a Masters of Divinity or Masters of Education Degree while offering guidance and teaching the younger generations. Craig resides in Clinton, Maryland located in Prince George's County.